INFO BANK

SCIENCE

First published by Miles Kelly Publishing Ltd
Bardfield Centre, Great Bardfield
Essex, CM7 4SL

British Library Cataloguing-in-Publication Data
A catalogue record for this book is available from the British Library

ISBN 1-84236-152-X
Printed in Hong Kong

www.mileskelly.net
info@mileskelly.net

Acknowledgements

The publishers would like to thank the following artists whose work appears in this book:

Kuo Kang Chen, Nick Farmer/A Dab Hand Ltd, Nicholas Forder, Mike Foster /Maltings Partnership,
Peter Gregory, Alan Hancocks, Peter Harper, Aziz Khan, Janos Marffy, Peter Sarson,
Martin Sanders, Mike Saunders, Guy Smith /Mainline Design, Rudi Vizi,
Mike White/Temple Rogers,Tony Wilkins, Paul Williams, John Woodcock.

The publishers would like to thank the following sources for the photographs used in this book:

P10-11 (B/R) Roger Ressmeyer/Corbis; P18-19 (B/R) NASA; P22-23 (B/R) John H Clark/Corbis;
P64-65 (R) NASA/Corbis; P76-77 (T/L) Bettmann/Corbis; P84-85 (C) David Arky/Corbis;
P86-87 (C) Nasa; P88-89 (C) Richard Cummins/Corbis
Thanks to Sony Computer Entertainment Europe

All other photographs from Miles Kelly archives.

INFO BANK

SCIENCE

STEVE PARKER

Miles Kelly
PUBLISHING

CONTENTS

POWER

MOTION

MACHINES

ENERGY

WAVES

SCIENTIFIC SUBJECTS

Materials

Plastics are light, durable and colourful. But a plastic bowl melts over flames. Like all materials, plastics have limits. Metals and glass withstand flames better, but glass shatters when knocked hard. Composites are materials mixed specially for particular jobs.

States

Iron is solid. Water is liquid. Oxygen is gas. Usually. But they can all change their forms, or states. Water freezes at 0°C into solid ice. With enough heat from burning fuel, iron melts into a liquid at 1535°C. Even hotter is matter's fourth state, plasma, where particles called ions have electric charges.

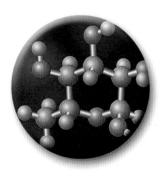

Matter

Keep splitting a substance into pieces. How far can you get? Molecules like DNA are collections of atoms. There are 115-plus kinds of atoms, such as carbon, iron and oxygen. Each is a chemical element. Atoms are made of sub-atomic particles, chiefly electrons, protons and neutrons. Smaller still are quarks.

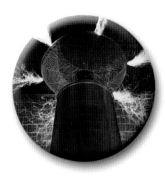

Electricity
One of the smallest particles is the electron. Billions of them flowing along are convenient, useful energy – electricity. We measure it accurately, alter and manipulate it in many ways, from microchips to power stations, and change or convert it to other forms of energy such as light, heat and sound.

Chemical change
Our world is composed of atoms, which make up chemicals, which change in reactions. Sometimes they join, in other cases they split, often helped by extra substances called catalysts. Biochemicals – like those in the body – do this every second, as we breathe air and slow-burn or combust it, for energy.

Power
In everyday life 'power' usually means generated electricity, most notably when it fails, in a power cut. In science, power is using energy or doing work over time. Rockets and other engines, burning fuel, splitting the nucleus of an atom, and light or heat from the Sun, are all further meanings of the term 'power'.

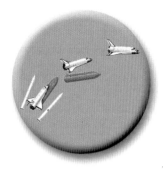

Motion
Moving in straight lines and circles, rotating or spinning, and being pushed or pulled by forces like gravity, are all governed by basic physical laws. Scientists calculate motion very carefully, so that a funfair ride stays safe and a shuttle reaches space.

Machines
A machine makes tasks easier. A simple lever lifts the lid off a can. A wheel lets a weight roll. Pulleys or gears move a big load with a small force. Hydraulics use pressure in liquids to the same effect. But the laws of mechanics do not allow something for nothing. The bigger the load, the less it moves.

Energy
The ability to make things happen, cause change, and do work – this is energy. It takes dozens of forms such as sound, heat, light, motion, electricity, and radioactivity from the splitting of the centres, or nuclei, of atoms. Energy can happen in bursts or pulses, like the 'pieces' of light known as photons.

Waves

To and fro, up-down, in-out – energy moves as waves of many kinds. We use the range or spectrum of electromagnetic (EM) waves every day, including radio waves, microwaves, light in all its colours, X-rays and many other kinds of radiation.

HOW TO USE THE SUBJECT LINKS

Navigate your way through this book using the colour-coded lozenges located in the bottom right hand corner of every spread. Flip through the pages, matching colours and sub-headings, and you can compare and contrast topics such as atoms in action, astronomy and in flight across ten different scientific areas.

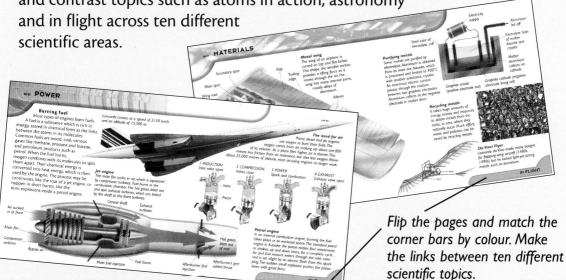

Flip the pages and match the corner bars by colour. Make the links between ten different scientific topics.

Plastics

Most plastics are made from petroleum (crude oil). They are lightweight, waterproof, tough and hard-wearing, do not rot or decay and resist the passage of heat and electricity. They can be made in a vast variety of colours which are see-through or not, and can be shaped or moulded into almost any form, with smooth surfaces and non-sharp edges. These features make plastics ideal for cases, components and other items, especially for electrical equipment such as computers, games consoles, hi-fi systems and kitchen appliances.

Stamping and pressing
A block of plastic is pressed hard and fast into the required shape.

Moulding
Molten, runny plastic is poured into a shaped mould. As it cools it goes solid and hard.

Injection
Plastic is forced or injected by a heating and screw device into a hollow shape, the mould, where it takes on the shape and then sets hard.

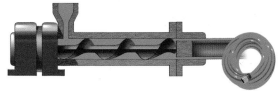

Extrusion
Plastic is heated, pressurized and then squeezed. and stretched or drawn through a narrow gap, to form a long, continuous part such as a pipe, tube or rod.

Practical plastic

Nearly all parts of the handset and console are moulded from plastics of different types and colours. They are strong, light and do not conduct electricity and so form a safe exterior.

Early plastics

In about 1907 Belgian-American chemist, Leo Baekeland (1863-1944) studied the chemical reactions between substances such as phenol and formaldehyde. He produced a dark substance that set hard when cool and did not conduct electricity. Named Bakelite, this early plastic was soon being shaped into frames and casings for electrical items.

Permanent plastic

Some types of plastic would last in nature for hundreds of years. However this poses problems of waste and pollution. Biodegradeable plastic items are made so after they have finished their useful life they decay or rot naturally, by the action of fungi and bacteria.

Purpose-made combinations

A composite is a material made from a combination of other single substances, such as metal, glass, plastic or fibre. Glass may be very hard and stiff, but if it is bent too much, it cracks and shatters. Plastic can bend much more easily, but it is not very hard. Add the two together and the resulting composite, glass-reinforced plastic, has the main benefits of both its ingredients. Composites are purpose-made for special uses, by mixing ingredients in certain proportions.

Based on carbon

Many composites are based on the element (pure chemical substance) carbon. An atom of carbon has four available links, to join or bond with up to four other atoms. What makes carbon special is that it links easily to itself, forming long chains, circles, pyramids and even spheres all made out of carbon atoms.

Composite blades

A wind generator turns the kinetic energy of moving air into electricity. Its blades or rotors must have the right amount of flexibility. Too stiff, and they would snap in a powerful wind. Too bendy, and they might kink or crack. So they are made from a specially designed composite such as carbon-fibre plastic.

Carbon-fibre composite

Carbon fibres are black, silky strands of pure carbon, with the atoms linked together into very long chains. They resist the stresses of being pulled or stretched, much better than steel. Carbon-fibre composites have hundreds of uses — from powerboat hulls, and the parts for jet planes and racing cars, to tennis racquets.

Designing composites

Each composite is made as a prototype or test material, where scientists make an informed guess about the proportions of the different ingredients.

Metal

The grains or crystals of a metal give hardness to the composite. They also help to carry electricity. The more metal in a composite, the better it becomes as an electrical conductor.

Fibre

Hair-like fibres or filaments give flexibility to the composite, without allowing it to crack or snap. There are many kinds of fibres, made from carbon, plastic or even glass.

Ceramic

Ceramics are clay-based materials that are very hard, and also withstand great heat and chemicals. Tiny particles of ceramic make a composite tougher and less prone to overheating.

Composite composites

The streamlined bodywork of a racing car contains a mix of glass-fibres and carbon-fibres in plastic resins.

The composite

All the ingredients are brought together in combination. The way the fibres are arranged will affect whether the composite has bending strength in just one direction, or several directions. The ingredients may be spread through, or embedded in, a surrounding 'background' substance called a matrix. Plastics and resins are common as matrix materials.

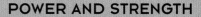

Liquid or solid?

Glass is difficult, not only to see, but also to describe. As a 'supercooled liquid', glass is like a clear liquid, similar to water, which has cooled enough to become almost solid. It hardly spreads or flows any more. Another description is 'amorphous solid', which refers to the lack of any patterns or structures in glass, on the microscopic or molecular scale. This absence of internal structure is one reason why glass cracks at almost any site and any angle.

Making glass

Here people are manufacturing a glass telecope. Most glass is made from the minerals silica (silicon dioxide, SiO_2, which makes up sand), sodium-containing soda ash, and calcium-containing limestone. These are heated in a furnace to about 1500°C. They melt and mix, and are then cooled.

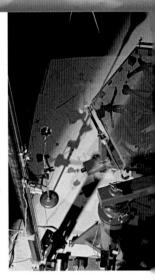

The first telescopes

Telescopes were probably invented in the Netherlands around 1600-1608. The first eminent scientist to study the night sky through one was Italian physicist and mathematician Galileo Galilei (1564-1642). By 1610 he had written descriptions of craters on the Moon, many stars too faint to see with the unaided eye, and also tiny moons orbiting the planet Jupiter. This last discovery showed that not everything in the Universe went around the Earth, as was then believed. It gradually led to a revolution in science.

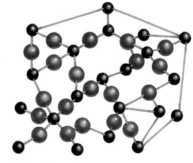

Inside glass

As glassy minerals are heated, they melt and their atoms and molecules are free to move. As they cool they do not have time to take up an ordered, regular pattern. They 'freeze' in random positions as an amorphous solid.

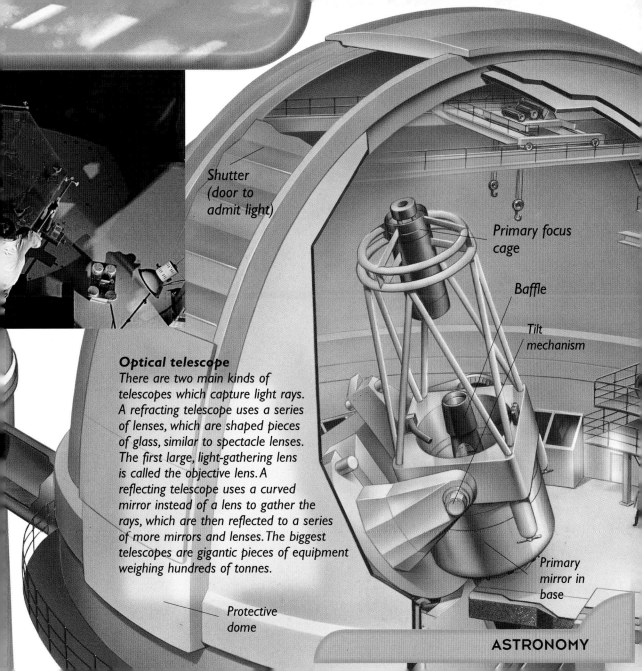

Shutter
(door to
admit light)

Primary focus
cage

Baffle

Tilt
mechanism

Optical telescope
There are two main kinds of
telescopes which capture light rays.
A refracting telescope uses a series
of lenses, which are shaped pieces
of glass, similar to spectacle lenses.
The first large, light-gathering lens
is called the objective lens. A
reflecting telescope uses a curved
mirror instead of a lens to gather the
rays, which are then reflected to a series
of more mirrors and lenses. The biggest
telescopes are gigantic pieces of equipment
weighing hundreds of tonnes.

Primary
mirror in
base

Protective
dome

ASTRONOMY

MATERIALS

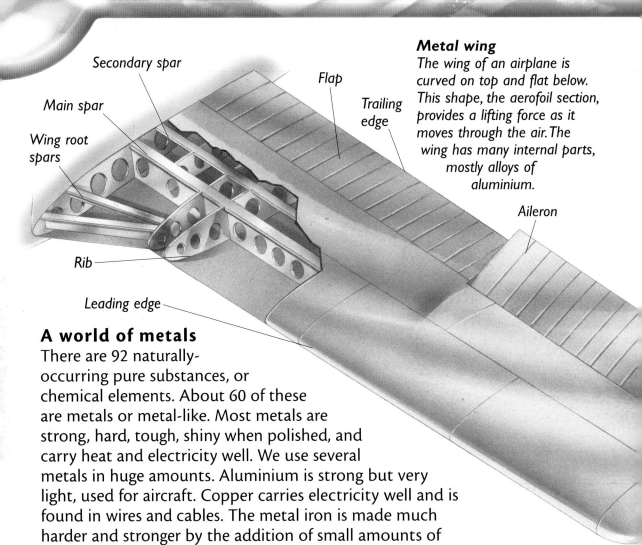

Secondary spar

Main spar

Wing root spars

Rib

Leading edge

Flap

Trailing edge

Metal wing
The wing of an airplane is curved on top and flat below. This shape, the aerofoil section, provides a lifting force as it moves through the air. The wing has many internal parts, mostly alloys of aluminium.

Aileron

A world of metals

There are 92 naturally-occurring pure substances, or chemical elements. About 60 of these are metals or metal-like. Most metals are strong, hard, tough, shiny when polished, and carry heat and electricity well. We use several metals in huge amounts. Aluminium is strong but very light, used for aircraft. Copper carries electricity well and is found in wires and cables. The metal iron is made much harder and stronger by the addition of small amounts of the non-metal element, carbon. The resulting 'mixture', or alloy, is known as steel. It has thousands of uses.

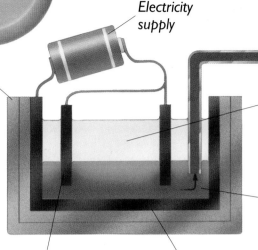

Electricity supply

Steel case of electrolytic cell

Aluminium led off

Electrolyte bath of molten bauxite and cryolite

Molten aluminium collects on cathode

Graphite anode (positive electrode rod)

Graphite cathode (negative electrode lining cell)

Purifying metals

Some metals are purified by electrolysis. Aluminium is obtained from its main ore, bauxite, which is processed and heated to 900°C with another substance, cryolite. An enormous electric current passes through the mixture between two graphite electrodes. Aluminium collects at the negative electrode in molten form.

Recycling metals

It takes huge amounts of energy, money and resources to obtain metals from the rocks, or ores, where they naturally occur. Much effort, waste and pollution can be saved by recycling metals.

Da Vinci Flyer

Leonardo da Vinci made many designs for flapping-wing aircraft (1480s-1490s) but he lacked light-yet-strong metals such as aluminium.

Go with the flow

Water changes shape as it flows from one place to another. So do oil, alcohol and petrol. These are all liquids. A liquid, like a gas, is a fluid. It can move, spread out under the downward pull of gravity, and change shape to fit its container. But unlike a gas, a liquid does not expand to fill every part of its container. Neither can a liquid be squeezed or compressed as easily as a gas. A liquid tends to remain the same volume.

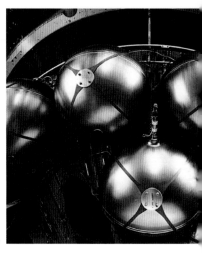

The fuel tanks of the US Skylab space station (launched in 1973) were made of titanium metal.

Water on the Moon

There is no liquid water on the Moon, as the Apollo astronauts discovered during their explorations between 1969 and 1972. However discoveries during the 1990s suggested that there could be water frozen into ice under the surface, actually inside the rocks of the Moon. Since water is vital to life, this raises the possibility that some types of simple life-forms once survived on the Moon.

Liquid fuel

When a gas changes into a liquid, it takes up much less space – perhaps thousands of times less. So cooling and compressing a gas into liquid is an efficient way of storing it. Many rocket engines carry fuel, or propellant, as a liquid. The tanks which contain the liquid are made of very strong, hard metal, such as titanium, to withstand great temperature and pressure. The liquid changes into gas as it feeds into the engine.

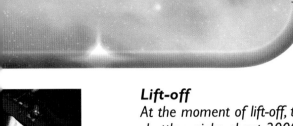

Lift-off

At the moment of lift-off, the entire space shuttle weighs about 2000 tonnes. Some 710 tonnes are liquid hydrogen and liquid oxygen, intensely cooled and under great pressure in the huge brown external fuel tank.

The liquid state

A liquid's atoms and molecules are free to move about in relation to each other. But they stay at the same distance apart from each other. So the liquid tends not to expand or contract, unless its temperature changes. As it gets warmer, its atoms and molecules move very slightly farther apart, and also begin to move faster. So the liquid expands slightly, and heat or convection currents are set up within it which spread out the heat energy.

Weightless liquid

On the surface of the Earth, the force of gravity pulls a liquid downwards. In the weightless conditions of space, it floats freely. Without the one-sided pull of gravity, each blob forms a perfect sphere.

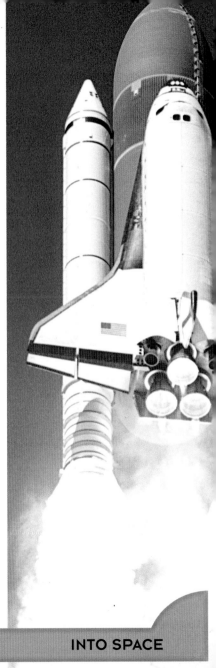

Hot and electric

The three familiar states of matter are solid, liquid and gas. But there is a fourth state – plasma. It usually occurs only at very high temperatures, generally thousands of degrees Celsius. A plasma is an ionized gas – a gas which contains ions. This means it is a gas in which the atoms, which normally have no electric charge, have become ions, which do have an electric charge, either positive or negative. (Ions occur much more commonly in liquids, when a substance such as sodium chloride or common salt dissolves, to form positive sodium ions and negative chloride ions.)

Where plasmas are found
Temperatures high enough to form plasmas are found under special conditions here on Earth, both natural and man-made, and also in various places out in space, such as inside stars. One example is the auroras called the Northern and Southern Lights, which are vast, glowing, rippling curtains of light high in the sky, near the North and South Poles. A sudden flash of lightning can also heat the air next to it to form plasma, for a split second.

Aurora
3500°C

Electric lights
Up to 5000°C

Lightning
30,000°C

The fourth state of matter

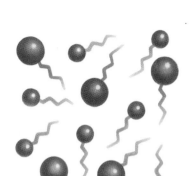

Plasma consists of atoms which move very fast indeed, and freely, as in a gas, to fill up the space they are allowed. However the atoms have lost or gained particles called electrons. Those that have lost electrons, which are negative, become positive. Atoms which gain electrons are negative. These electrically charged versions of atoms are known as ions.

Nebula
25,000 to 50,000°C

Sun's corona
6000°C

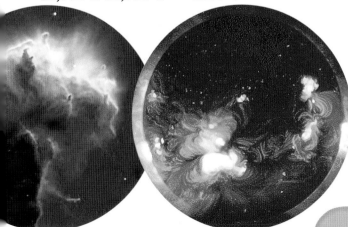

Power from plasma

Normal nuclear power is obtained by fission, which is splitting the nuclei (centres) of atoms. Another possibility is fusion, where nuclei are pressed together so that they fuse or join. Plasma fusion power (above) is being researched, but the practical problems are huge. The plasma fuel must be heated so much that it cannot be kept in place by a container, since its walls would melt. So it has to be confined by intense magnetism, which uses more energy than is obtained from fusion in the plasma.

Vital but invisible

There are gases all around us. If there were not, we would die. Air is a mixture of several invisible gases. The main one is nitrogen, which makes up about four-fifths of air. Next is oxygen, which is vital for our bodily life processes, and which we take in by breathing. There are also small amounts of other gases, chiefly argon, also carbon dioxide, neon, helium, krypton, xenon and ozone.

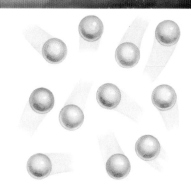

Compressing air

As a gas is forced into a smaller container, its atoms or molecules become closer together, and the gas's pressure rises. They also bump into each other more often, so the gas's temperature rises too. Air is compressed like this when it is pumped into a tyre, which is why the tyre becomes hot.

The gaseous state
Like a liquid, a gas 'flows'. Its atoms or molecules can move about freely at high speed. However, they are much farther apart, and travel much faster, in a gas than in a liquid. Given more space, they spread out even farther.

Gas fuels

Some gases are made of molecules which contain plenty of chemical energy in the bonds between their atoms. Examples include methane (CH_4), ethane (C_2H_6) and propane (C_3H_8). These are burned as fuels for engines and heating. They are compressed so much, for storage in tanks (right), that they turn from gas into liquid.

Emergency

If an aircraft leaks, its gases rapidly flow away and the airplane 'depressurizes'. So an emergency system provides vital oxygen from cylinders, for breathing through masks.

Extra back-up oxygen cylinders

Oxygen pipes

Oxygen cylinders

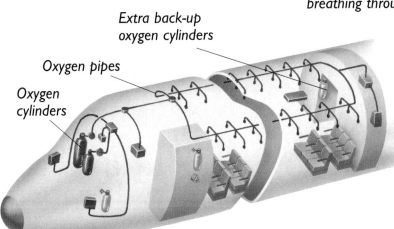

Life-saving gas

As you travel higher, away from Earth's surface, the air becomes thinner with less oxygen, and colder, and lower in pressure. This would be very dangerous for the human body. So high-flying airplanes are sealed airtight, and the gases inside kept at the correct oxygen content, temperature and pressure for comfort.

Not enough gas

Before aircraft were pressurized, they had to fly lower and battle through clouds, rain, wind and other weather, which occur mainly below heights of 6000 metres. From the 1940s, pressurized aircraft such as the Boeing Stratoliner and Lockheed Constellation (below) could fly higher, faster and more smoothly 'above the weather'.

IN FLIGHT

Colours of solids

For objects which do not make their own light, like guitars, loudspeakers and performers, their colour depends on the colours of light which they absorb. The solid surface of the loudspeaker absorbs all the light which falls on it, and reflects very little, which is why it is black.

The solid state

The wood of a guitar, its metal strings and its plastic trim are all types of solids. The atoms in a solid are close together, fixed in position by chemical bonds and other forces. But each one can move or vibrate slightly around a central point – its 'average' position.

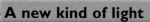

A new kind of light

American scientist Theodore Maiman (1927-) made the first working laser in 1960. He used a rod-shaped ruby crystal which produced red light. Laser light differs from ordinary light in three ways. First, its beam does not spread out or disperse. Second, all its waves are the same length, and so the same pure colour. Third, all the waves are in step, their peaks in line. These features give laser light great power.

Laser light

A source of energy, such as ordinary light from a flash tube, is fed into an active medium – a crystal such as ruby. As more energy is 'pumped' in, the energy levels rise in the atoms. Suddenly all the atoms give out excess energy as a flash of laser light.

Unchanging shapes

A substance which stays the same shape, and does not alter or flow, is a solid. Its atoms are arranged in a certain pattern, and hardly move about in relation to each other. Some solids are very hard and tough, like most metals and rocks. Others can change shape when squeezed or stretched, like rubber, elastic and some types of plastic. But they do not spread out and flow from place to place, like a liquid or gas.

Crystals

In some solids, the atoms have a pattern or arrangement that repeats itself many times, like bricks in a wall. The larger the solid object, the more of these repeating units it contains. This structure gives the whole solid object a certain shape, with flat sides or faces, and sharp edges. These types of solids are called crystals.

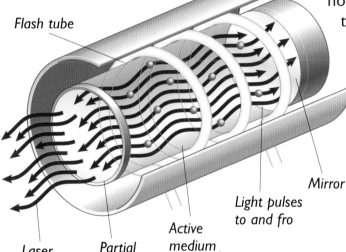

Flash tube

Mirror

Light pulses to and fro

Active medium

Partial mirror

Laser beam

Quartz

Galena

Pyrite

Gypsum

Barite

Calcite

Smaller and smaller

What makes up the Universe? What does matter – from a grain of sand, to a human body, to the Earth or a star – consist of? One idea was that all matter contained tiny building-blocks called atoms. They were the smallest particles, and could not be split further. However, in the early 20th century, atoms were split. They were made of even smaller particles, chiefly protons, neutrons and electrons. In the middle of the 20th century it became clear that some of these sub-atomic particles were composed of yet smaller particles, such as quarks. How do we know? We blast apart these tiny objects in particle-accelerators or 'atom-smashers'.

Detector
Particles collide or smash together in detectors, which are like giant, fast-action electronic cameras.

Bits and pieces

The two main groups of fundamental particles are quarks and leptons. There are six kinds or 'flavours' of quarks: up, down, bottom, top, strange and charm. A proton is two up and one down quarks; a neutron is one up and two down quarks. The six kinds of leptons include the electron.

CERN
This accelerator under the Swiss-French border. has a tunnel 27 kilometres long.

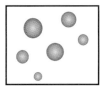

leptons   **quarks**

Aerial view of the CERN ring-shaped particle accelerator

Electromagnets

These are switched on and off to give extra energy to the particles inside their tubes, and speed them on their way.

Big rings

The largest particle accelerators are by far the world's biggest machines – huge tunnels usually under the ground. The particles are given off by very hot, electrified filaments of metals and other substances. The ring structure means the particles can go round and round, faster every time, until diverted by more magnets into the detectors.

Tunnel structure

An accelerator usually has two tunnels, one inside the other. The inner tunnel has no air – it is a vacuum so the particles can move at maximum speed.

Small idea

The idea of all matter being made of tiny particles goes back to Ancient Greece. The thinker Democritus (who lived about 470-400 BC) suggested that the Universe was a vast area of nothing, with atoms scattered about. He believed that each atom was too small to see, too hard to split or break, and lasted for ever.

ATOMS IN ACTION

Electrons and microchips

A microchip is a thin wafer or sliver of germanium, silicon or a similar element that may or may not conduct electrons, depending on the conditions. Such elements are known as semiconductors. Micro-components are formed on the semiconductor and linked to create circuits.

Atoms and electrons

The smallest chemical units of matter are atoms. Once an atom of a chemical element is split apart, its sub-atomic particles no longer have the properties of the original element. In fact, each type of sub-atomic particle is the same in all atoms. Electrons in a carbon atom are the same as electrons in atoms of iron, aluminium, sulphur, sodium and all other elements. Likewise for the protons, and the neutrons. Electrons are especially important sub-atomic particles because they can 'hop' from one atom to another, forming an electric current. They can also pass through air or a vacuum, as electron beams.

Electronic circuits

In a typical piece of electrical equipment, many microchips, resistors, capacitors and other components are joined by wires to form circuits that manipulate electrons and so electric currents. The metal wires and strips that connect the components are put onto a non-conducting baseboard, by a process which is similar to printing inks onto paper. The boards are known as printed circuit boards.

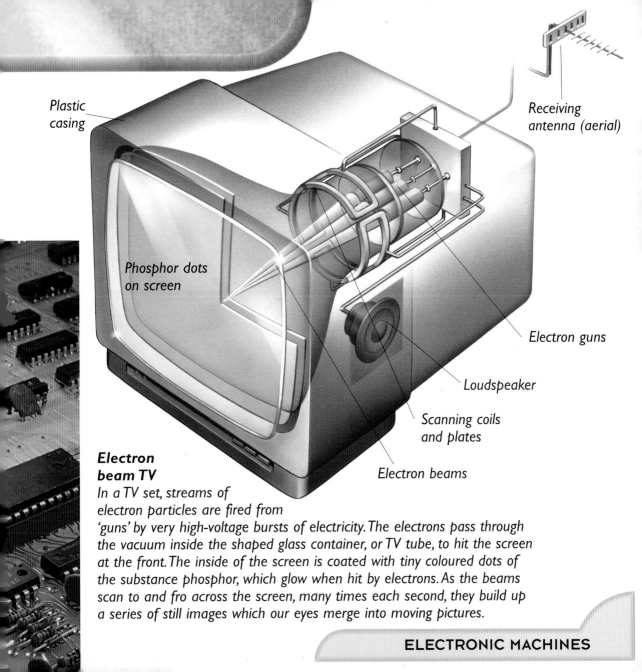

Plastic casing

Receiving antenna (aerial)

Phosphor dots on screen

Electron guns

Loudspeaker

Scanning coils and plates

Electron beams

Electron beam TV

In a TV set, streams of electron particles are fired from 'guns' by very high-voltage bursts of electricity. The electrons pass through the vacuum inside the shaped glass container, or TV tube, to hit the screen at the front. The inside of the screen is coated with tiny coloured dots of the substance phosphor, which glow when hit by electrons. As the beams scan to and fro across the screen, many times each second, they build up a series of still images which our eyes merge into moving pictures.

ELECTRONIC MACHINES

Elements in DNA

The substance DNA (de-oxyribonucleic acid), which carries the body's genetic instructions, is made of millions of atoms. But these are from only five elements — carbon, hydrogen, oxygen, nitrogen and phosphorus. The atoms are arranged in subgroups and strung together as two long 'backbones' twisted around each other, with cross-links between the backbones.

Double-helix

Backbone

Information coded in sequences of cross-links

The number of elements

There are 92 elements which occur naturally, and another 25 or so which have been created artificially by scientists. They vary from soft white metals such as calcium, to hard, dense metals like iron. Under the microscope, some resemble fibres or strings, while others are jagged-edged crystals.

Same and different

There are untold trillions of atoms. But there are only a limited number of different kinds, or types, of atoms. Each kind has a certain number of protons and neutrons in its nucleus, with a certain number of electrons going around the nucleus. These atom 'types' are known as chemical elements. Examples of elements include carbon, oxygen, nitrogen, iron, sulphur, chlorine, sodium and gold. All atoms of an element, such as carbon, are the same as each other, and different from the atoms of all other elements.

Elements in the body

The most common elements in the body, by weight, are the most common elements in most biochemicals – oxygen, carbon and hydrogen. Molecules made from atoms of these three elements alone are known as carbohydrates. The element calcium is an important part of teeth and bones, giving strength and toughness.

1 Oxygen 65%   4 Nitrogen 3.2%
2 Carbon 18.5%   5 Calcium 1.5%
3 Hydrogen 9.5%   6 Others 2.3%

Typical living cell

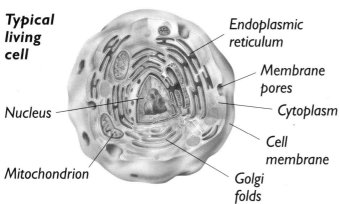

Nucleus

Mitochondrion

Endoplasmic reticulum

Membrane pores

Cytoplasm

Cell membrane

Golgi folds

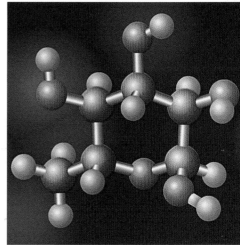

Energy for cells

The major energy source for cells, to power their life processes, is the sugar molecule, glucose. This is a carbohydrate, made of just 24 atoms from three elements – carbon, hydrogen and oxygen ($C_6H_{12}O_6$).

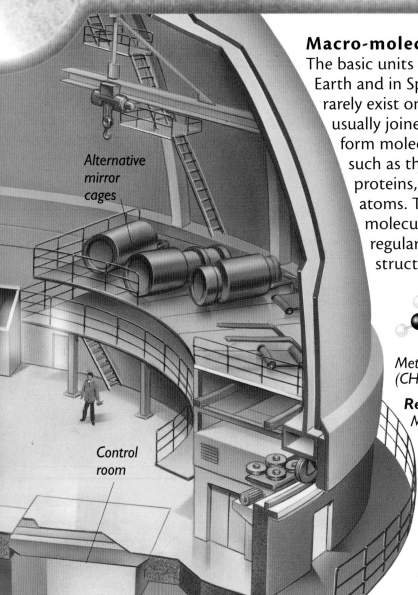

Alternative mirror cages

Control room

Macro-molecules

The basic units of matter, both here on Earth and in Space, are atoms. But they rarely exist on their own. They are usually joined to other atoms, to form molecules. Certain molecules, such as those in plastics and proteins, each have thousands of atoms. They are called macro-molecules, and usually have a regular pattern or repeating structure.

Methane
(CH_4)

Butane
(CH_3-CH_3)

Ethene
$(CH_2=CH_2)$

Repeating structure

Many macro-molecules are built around the two elements of carbon and oxygen, and are known as organic hydrocarbons. They include gases such as methane and butane. Some are made up of repeating units of one carbon and two hydrogen atoms, -CH$_2$- .

Bright and hot

The H-R (Hertzsprung-Russell) diagram is a graph that compares the brightness of stars, with their colours. The colour of a star shows its temperature, since cooler stars are red, medium-hot ones are yellow, and very hot stars are white or blue. Most stars form a line on the chart called the Main Sequence. Red giant stars and white dwarf stars form separate groups.

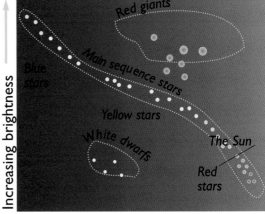

Molecules from space

How did life begin on Earth? One idea was that life did not start here. Simple life-forms appeared somewhere else in the Universe, and travelled to Earth on a long-distance space wanderer such as a comet or asteroid.

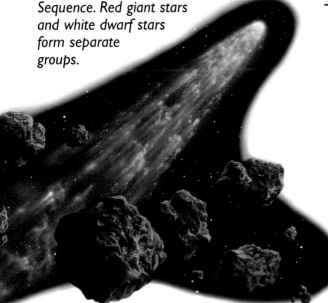

Martian molecules

In the early 1990s scientists studied a meteorite which came from Mars. The microscope revealed tiny sausage-like shapes, each hundreds of times thinner than a human hair. One explanation was that they were micro-fossils – preserved remains of microbes. This meant life on Mars! Another explanation was that they were minerals, created by natural rock-forming processes.

Energy to make electricity

Various sources of energy can be converted into electricity. The commonest form is chemical energy, in fuels such as coal, oil (petroleum), natural gas and wood. This is burned to form heat energy, which spins turbines as kinetic (movement) energy, which is finally converted by a generator into electrical energy.

Power station

Moving electrons

Current electricity exists as moving electrons, which are particles normally found in the outer parts of atoms. In certain substances, especially metals, the outermost electrons can detach easily from their atoms. They jump or hop to nearby atoms. Billions of electrons all hopping in the same direction, from atom to atom, create an electric current.

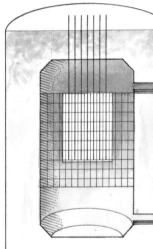

Nuclear reactor

Plastic coating

Wires and cables are coated with plastic insulation. This plastic coating protects the wire and is also flexible enough to allow the wire to be bent into any shape.

Insulating plastic cover

Nuclear power

Heat is given off as the nuclei (centres) of atoms break apart.

Current electricity

Static electricity is like still water, held behind a dam, ready to flow somewhere. Electricity that moves or flows along, like water in a river, is known as current electricity. It is a very powerful and adaptable form of energy. One of its main features is that it can be transported from place to place, by sending it along wires or cables. Also it can be changed or converted into many other forms of energy, including sound, light and heat.

Alternating current

The electricity made by power stations is alternating current, AC. The direction of the current goes one way, then flows the other way, then reverses again, and so on.

Transmitting electricity

The electricity made by the generator is carried through cables called power lines. They are buried underground or held up on tall towers, for safety.

Transforming electricity

Before feeding electric current to the main power lines, its voltage (pushing strength) is boosted to hundreds of thousands of volts, by a device called a transformer. This allows the current to travel long distances along power lines without losing too much of its energy, especially as heat.

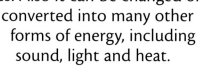

Heat exchanger

Transformer

Turbines

Generator

Secondary circuit of hot water

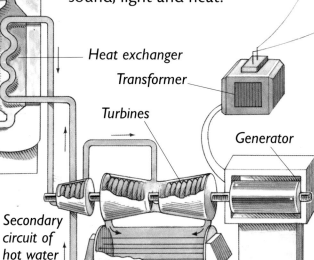

POWER AND STRENGTH

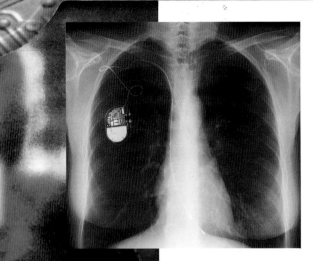

Signals to the heart
In some heart problems, the impulses of electricity which control the heart's beating are not produced properly. So an artificial pacemaker may be put under the skin, to generate electrical signals for the heart.

The electric body
Electricity can be converted into many other forms of energy – and the reverse. A handy example of these conversions at work is the human body. In fact, a major system of the body, the nervous system, is based on electricity. Millions of tiny electrical pulses pass along the network of nerves that branches through all body parts, and also to, from and within the brain. The pulses are termed nerve signals or nervous impulses and they represent thoughts, memories and sensations.

Whole body scan (left)

Axon terminal

Electrical cell
The nerve cell or neurone is specialized to pass on nerve signals. It receives signals from other cells through its short, branched dendrites, which may number many thousand. The signals pass through the long, wire-like axon, and are then transmitted to other cells.

Passing on electro-signals

A nerve cell is separated from other nerve cells by tiny gaps known as synapses. When a nerve signal reaches a synapse, it converts to chemical form – biochemicals called neurotransmitters. These cross the synapse in a split second and generate a nerve signal in the receiving cell.

Sending cell

Neuro-transmitters

Receiving cell

Seeing nerve signals

Delicate medical equipment can detect the tiny electrical pulses of nerve signals, or their effects, and strengthen them enough to display on a screen or paper strip. The pulses are usually picked up by sensors placed on the skin.

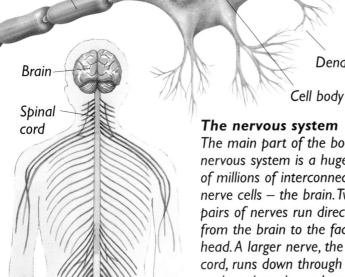

Cell nucleus

Axon

Dendrites

Cell body

Brain

Spinal cord

The nervous system

The main part of the body's nervous system is a huge 'lump' of millions of interconnected nerve cells – the brain. Twelve pairs of nerves run directly from the brain to the face and head. A larger nerve, the spinal cord, runs down through the neck and sends out branches to all body parts.

HUMAN BODY

Units

The pushing strength of an electric current is known as potential difference and is measured in volts. It is like the pressure of water flowing through a pipe. The quantity of electricity is called its current and is measured in amps. Any obstacle or narrow part that the electricity tries to pass is known as resistance, and is measured in ohms.

Current – amps

Potential difference – volts

Resistance – ohms

Electron

Atom

Electron hops to next atom

In a wire

Substances that carry electricity well are known as conductors. Most metals are good conductors. They have atoms with just one or two outermost electrons. These can easily detach from their atom and jump to the next one. When millions of electrons do this, their flow is an electric current.

To the home

Electricity arrives in a neighbourhood along huge power lines which carry hundreds of thousands of volts. Before use, the voltage is lowered, or stepped down, by devices known as transformers.

Transformer

Push and power

Water flowing in a river can be measured in several ways. Quantity is the amount of water flowing past one place over a certain time. Pressure is the pushing force of the water. Electricity is similar to water in the way it is measured. It has a pushing force, a rate of flow, and other features which can be given numbers. This is vital when planning electrical equipment, from a microchip as small as this 'o' to the distribution grid for a whole country.

Electron in outermost shell

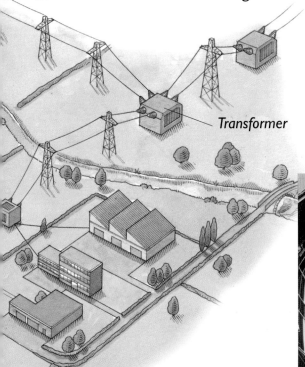

Transformer

Metal atom

Like most metals, uranium carries electricity well. Each of its atoms (above) has lots of electrons, but only two in its outermost layer or shell. These can move fairly easily, and as they hop from one uranium atom to another, they form an electric current.

Magnets and coils of a huge electricity generator.

ATOMS IN ACTION

Manipulating

Electricity is a useful form of energy, partly because it can be altered and manipulated in many ways, by a range of electrical devices and electronic components. A capacitor stores electric charge. A resistor makes the flow of electricity weaker. An amplifier makes it stronger. An electric current can flow steadily in one direction, which is DC, direct current. Or it can flow one way, then the other, then the first way, and so on, reversing 50 or 60 times each second. This is AC, alternating current.

Effects of static

There are two kinds of electrostatic charge, positive and negative. Like ones repel, unlike ones attract. If like charges build up on objects, including hairs, they repel each other, causing a hair-raising effect.

Moving and still

Electricity flows along a wire as electrodynamic charge. If it has nowhere to flow, it collects on the surface of an object as electrostatic charge (static electricity). Van de Graaff generators (left) build up charges of millions of volts, which finally leap away as giant sparks.

Transistor

Battery current flows through these two layers

Bigger
A microphone produces tiny electrical pulses that vary with the sounds it receives. These signals are not strong enough to power a loudspeaker. But as the signals pass through a transistor, they can manipulate the much stronger electricity from a battery, in the same pattern as themselves. The increased or amplified signals then drive the loudspeaker.

Microphone signals flow through these two layers

Loudspeaker

Larger electrical signals from battery

Tiny electrical signals from microphone

Stronger electricity
An amplifier is a device which amplifies, or strengthens, electrical signals. It is the electronic version of a mechanical lever. It takes a series of small electrical signals, and uses these to control a larger electric current. The smaller set of signals manipulates the larger current to make the same pattern of signals, but greater in strength.

Replica of an early transistor (1947)

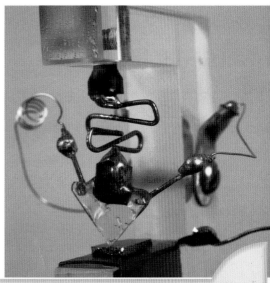

ELECTRONIC MACHINES

Living chemical factories

A living thing such as the human body is a vast collection of millions of chemicals, and they are changing and reacting all the time. Substances that are found particularly in living things are termed biochemicals, and many of them are the same throughout the living world. For example, the sugar glucose is made by plants, as they trap light energy from the Sun by photosynthesis. Almost all animals, including humans, use glucose too, as a ready source of energy – it is called 'blood sugar'.

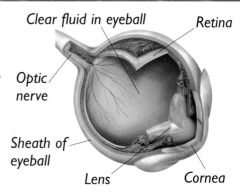

Clear fluid in eyeball
Retina
Optic nerve
Sheath of eyeball
Lens
Cornea

Light and bio-change

Light shines onto a very thin layer inside the back of the eyeball, called the retina. Each of the 125 million cells in the retina contains millions of copies of the bio-molecule rhodopsin. When light hits rhodopsin, it causes the rhodopsin to change shape, and this in turn generates a nerve pulse which passes to the brain.

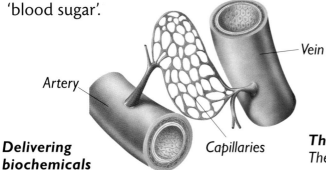

Artery

Vein

Capillaries

Delivering biochemicals

Arteries convey blood from the heart to every region. The arteries branch and divide many times until they are thinner than hairs, and known as capillaries. Glucose, oxygen and other vital biochemicals pass through the very thin walls of the capillaries, to the body's tissues and cells. The capillaries join to form wide veins which return the blood to the heart.

The ultimate biochemical

The instructions for how the body grows and develops, called genes, are in the form of biochemicals. They are known as DNA (de-oxyribonucleic acid). A molecule of DNA has a corkscrew-like shape, the double-helix.

Storing biochemicals

The largest organ (major part) inside the body is the liver. It stores many vital substances including vitamins and minerals. It also stores spare glucose from food by linking many molecules of it into a much larger bio-molecule, starch. If the body suddenly needs extra energy, the liver changes some of its starch into glucose and releases this into the blood stream.

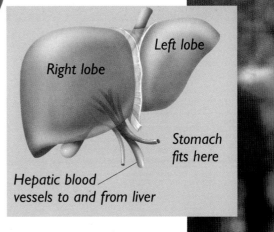

Right lobe

Left lobe

Stomach fits here

Hepatic blood vessels to and from liver

Red blood cells

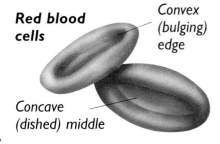

Convex (bulging) edge

Concave (dished) middle

Oxygen and biochemicals

Oxygen is absorbed through the lungs into the blood. It attaches to an iron-containing biochemical, haemoglobin, contained in red blood cells, for transport. There are five million red cells in a pinhead-sized drop of blood, and 270 million molecules of haemoglobin in each red cell. Away from the lungs, where levels of oxygen are lower, haemoglobin releases its oxygen for the cells and tissues.

Speeding up bio-reactions

Substances called catalysts can speed up or slow down chemical changes. The catalysts found in living things are called enzymes. The first person to make the pure form of an enzyme and study it was German bio-scientist Theodore Schwann (1810-1882), in about 1835. The enzyme is called pepsin and in the stomach it speeds up the breakdown and digestion of proteins in the food.

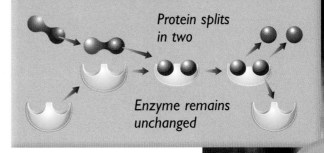

Protein splits in two

Enzyme remains unchanged

HUMAN BODY

Catalysts in fuel

Various catalysts are added to fuels, such as the rocket fuel in submarine-launched missiles. Some catalysts make the fuel reach full burning power very quickly. Others help the rocket engine to fire smoothly, without surges. The used or spent catalyst is blasted out of the rocket, along with the hot gases from the burn.

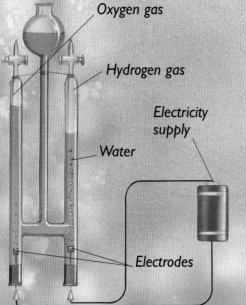

Oxygen gas

Hydrogen gas

Electricity supply

Water

Electrodes

Faster or slower

When two chemicals come together and change, or react, they do so at a certain rate. This depends partly on the nature of the chemicals themselves, and also on conditions such as temperature and pressure. However, the rate of reaction can be altered by another substance, called a catalyst. This 'helps' the reaction and may take part in it. But at the end, the catalyst has not been altered, and is the same as at the start.

Making air

A submarine stays underwater for months. Chemical systems on board refresh the air. Catalysts remove dangerous gases such as carbon dioxide and carbon monoxide. Vital oxygen is made by electrolysis — passing electricity through a liquid such as water, to split its molecules and release oxygen as a gas for breathing.

Fresh water from salty

Salty water can be changed into fresh by desalination. Sea water is heated and the water vapour ('steam') given off is collected and condensed – cooled back into liquid pure water – leaving salt behind. In practice, partly-heated sea water is passed through a low-pressure chamber, where the water boils at a lower temperature, lessening the need for heat energy. Desalination is used in submarines and in towns along the coasts of desert regions.

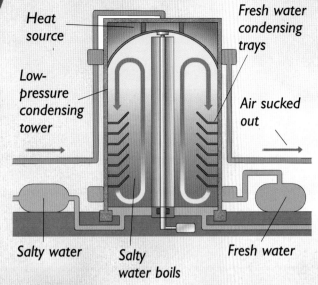

Heat source

Low-pressure condensing tower

Fresh water condensing trays

Air sucked out

Salty water

Salty water boils

Fresh water

Torpedo

The torpedo is a long, slim, self-powered weapon that races through the water towards an enemy target. One type has an explosive warhead near the front, a central control section, batteries, and an electric motor that spins the screws (propellers) at the rear. Sonar sensors at the front detect the sounds of an enemy vessel, and the torpedo adjusts its path so that the sounds become louder, until it reaches the target.

Batteries and electric motor

Control section with sonar analyzer and gyroscope

Main warhead

Contact detonator

SUBMARINE

Burns and blow-ups

Combustion is a special kind of chemical change. It is the rapid combination of a substance with oxygen. Usually, some of the energy in the chemical bonds of the substance is changed into heat and light, and the substance itself is drastically changed. Fairly slow combustion is known in everyday terms as burning. The light and heat are given off as flames. An explosion is very sudden, rapid combustion, with plenty of sound energy as well.

Ancient rockets

Gunpowder was one of the earliest substances to combust with explosive force. It was made as a mixture of minerals. Saltpetre (potassium nitrate) provided the oxygen, sulphur caught fire quickly, and powdered charcoal (carbon) burned hot and fiercely. This mixture may have been invented in China, some 1000 years ago, for use in rockets and bombs.

The colours of fireworks are usually based on different metal-containing chemicals

Fireworks

A fireworks rocket uses a modern type of gunpowder-based substance, a solid propellant. This burns very fast, but not quite with explosive suddenness. The smoke and hot gas products of combustion blast out of the base of the rocket and so thrust it forwards.

Nose cone

Solid propellant

Spark charge

Clay stopper

Outer casing

Fuse

Launch stick

Burning in air

In an ordinary flame, such as a gas burner, the oxygen comes from the air around. In a rocket or explosion, oxygen is provided by one of the chemicals in the mixture.

Coloured sparks

The shower of sparks from a firework is produced by combusting metal-containing chemicals with an explosive charge which blows up to spread them out. Magnesium-based chemicals give a very bright white light, while copper chemicals produce green or blue, and sodium gives yellow.

Atoms of magnesium, Mg, a silvery metal

Molecule of oxygen, O_2, in air

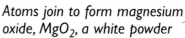

Atoms join to form magnesium oxide, MgO_2, a white powder

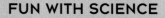

Inside an atom

An atom is made of three main kinds of particles. These are neutrons, protons and electrons. The protons and neutrons are close together in the atom's central 'lump', its nucleus. The electrons move around the nucleus. They do not travel at random, but in certain ball-shaped layers called shells. Electrons in different shells have different amounts of energy. Each pure substance or chemical element has its own number of protons, neutrons and electrons. The number of protons usually equals the number of electrons, and this is called the element's atomic number.

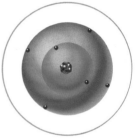

Carbon atom
*Nucleus with
6 protons*

Electron shell M

Electron shell L　　　*Nucleus*

Electron shell K

Chlorine atom
*Nucleus with
17 protons*

**Sodium
atom**
*Nucleus with
11 protons*

Oxygen atom
Nucleus with 8 protons

Plus equals minus
In an atom, the number of negative electrons usually balances the number of positive protons, so whole atom has no charge.

*7 electrons out of 8 in shell M
means that chlorine is drawn to
atoms with a spare electron*

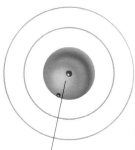

Single electron

Hydrogen atom
Nucleus with 1 proton

The first team of scientists to 'split the atom', from about 1919, was led by New Zealand-born physicist Ernest Rutherford (1871-1937). His early work involved radio waves and radioactivity. In 1911 he had suggested that an atom consists of several heavy particles in the middle, with lighter ones moving around them. This was the first fairly correct idea for the structure of an atom.

Ionic bonding

This involves the movement of one or a few electrons in the outermost shell. The electron jumps across to another atom which has a space in its outermost shell. The atom which has lost the negative electron now has a positive charge; the one which gains has a negative charge. When atoms have charges, they are called ions. Ions of different charges, positive and negative, attract and bond to each other.

Shared electrons

Covalent bonding

In this type of bonding an atom, with room in its outermost shell for an extra electron, gains such an electron by 'sharing' it with another atom. The electron repeatedly flips to and fro, first in one atom and then in the other.

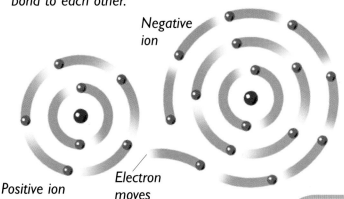

Negative ion

Positive ion

Electron moves

ATOMS IN ACTION

Burning fuel

Most types of engines burn fuels. A fuel is a substance which is rich in energy, stored in chemical form as the links between the atoms in its molecules. Common fuels are wood, coal, various gases like methane, propane and butane, and petroleum products such as petrol. When the fuel burns, oxygen combines with its molecules to split them apart. Their chemical energy is converted into heat energy, which is then used by the engine. The process may be continuous, like the roar of a jet engine, or happen in short bursts, like the mini-explosions inside a petrol engine.

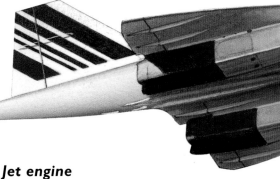

Concorde cruises at a speed of 2150 km/h and an altitude of 15,500 m

Jet engine
The main fan sucks in air, which is squeezed by compressor turbines. Fuel burns in the combustion chamber. The hot gases blast out and spin exhaust turbines, which are linked by the shaft to the front turbines.

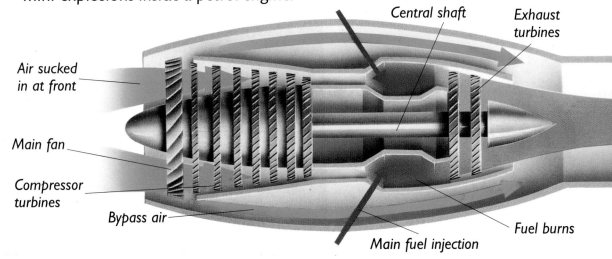

Central shaft

Exhaust turbines

Air sucked in at front

Main fan

Compressor turbines

Bypass air

Main fuel injection

Fuel burns

The need for air

Petrol, diesel and jet engines use oxygen to burn their fuels. The oxygen comes from air, making up about one-fifth of its volume. As a plane flies higher, air is thinner. This means less friction from air resistance, but also less oxygen. Above about 25,000 metres of altitude, most air-using engines no longer work.

1 INDUCTION
Inlet valve open

Valve

Piston

2 COMPRESSION
Valves close

3 POWER
Spark and combustion

4 EXHAUST
Exhaust valve open

Hot gases blast out of rear

Afterburner fuel injection

Afterburners give added thrust

Petrol engine

In an internal combustion engine, burning the fuel takes place in an enclosed space. The standard petrol engine is 4-stroke: the piston makes four movements or strokes, up and down twice, for a complete cycle. Air and fuel mixture enters through the inlet valve and is set alight by an electric flash from the spark plug. The sudden small explosion pushes the piston down with great force.

Rocket engine

A rocket engine works very simply, by burning fuel inside a heat-proof combustion chamber. The hot gases are directed to roar rearwards, out of the exhaust nozzle. Their action, pushing backwards, is accompanied by an equal and opposite reaction, pushing forwards the rocket engine and any objects attached to it. Like any engine which works by combustion, a rocket needs oxygen for its fuel, or propellant, to burn. In the vacuum of space, there is no oxygen. So the rocket takes its own, in the form of an oxidizer – a chemical which breaks down with heat to supply plentiful oxygen.

Early rockets

Apart from early gunpowder rockets, the first modern-style, liquid-fuel rocket flew in 1926. Its fuel was petrol (gasoline), and its oxidizer was liquid oxygen. Its designer was American scientist Robert Goddard (1882-1945). His first attempt reached a height of about 12 metres, but this soon improved. Goddard built bigger, more powerful rockets that sped to heights of 1500 metres and travelled faster than sound.

The shuttle set-up

The space shuttle is the world's only re-useable rocket system. The orbiter resembles a plane, with a length of 37.2 metres and a wing span of 23.8 metres. It has three rocket engines at its rear end. For the first part of the mission these are supplied with propellant and oxidizer by the giant fuel tank, which is 47 metres long. The two boosters have solid fuel and are used only for take-off.

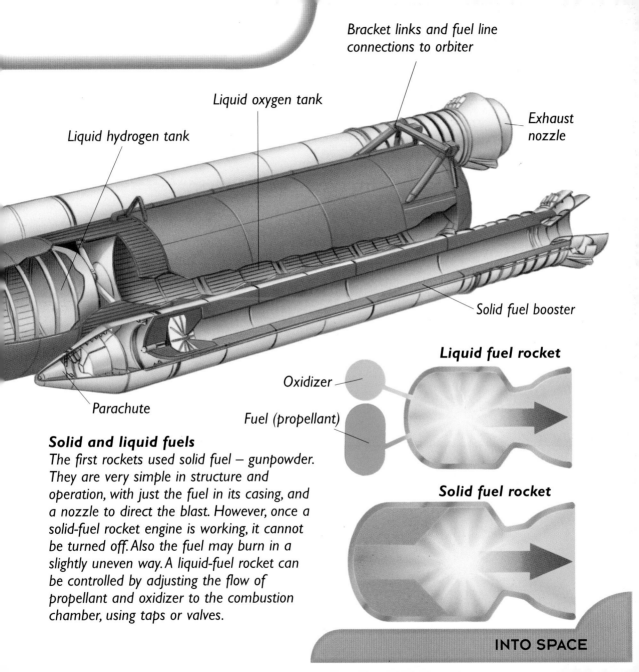

Bracket links and fuel line
connections to orbiter

Liquid oxygen tank

Exhaust
nozzle

Liquid hydrogen tank

Solid fuel booster

Parachute

Oxidizer

Fuel (propellant)

Liquid fuel rocket

Solid fuel rocket

Solid and liquid fuels

The first rockets used solid fuel – gunpowder.
They are very simple in structure and
operation, with just the fuel in its casing, and
a nozzle to direct the blast. However, once a
solid-fuel rocket engine is working, it cannot
be turned off. Also the fuel may burn in a
slightly uneven way. A liquid-fuel rocket can
be controlled by adjusting the flow of
propellant and oxidizer to the combustion
chamber, using taps or valves.

INTO SPACE

Screw
(propeller)

Rudders

Screw shaft

Main
gearbox

Turbo-generator
for sub's own
electricity supply

Central
shaft

Main
turbines

Back-up diesel
generator

Nuclear reactor

A nuclear reactor uses a fuel such as uranium, to produce a controlled chain reaction of nuclear splitting (fission). This generates heat, which is then used to spin turbines and generate electricity. Nuclear power stations have huge reactors. Smaller versions are used in submarines, where they have a great advantage over petrol or diesel engines: they do not use air.

Nuclear safety

A nuclear reaction produces various kinds of energy in addition to heat. Some of this energy is in the form of harmful radioactivity. Also, if the chain reaction gets out of control, it may happen so fast that it causes meltdown or even a nuclear explosion. So a nuclear reactor must be protected and shielded from its surroundings. Different types of nuclear reactions are tested in remote areas, like deserts, for safety reasons.

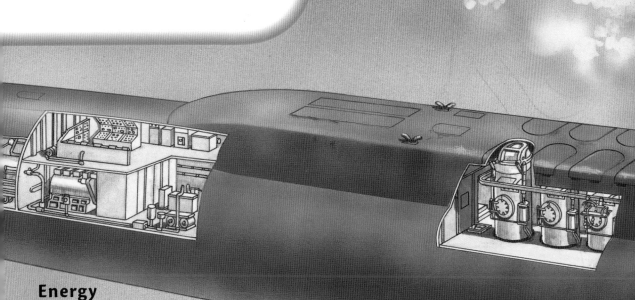

Energy from splitting

All matter is made of tiny pieces called atoms. At the centre of each atom is a nucleus, which is made of two types of sub-atomic particles, protons and neutrons. Certain types of atoms, like uranium, have nuclei which are unstable. These nuclei can be made to break or split, by bombarding them with other particles or energy. As each nucleus splits, some of its particles cease their existence as matter, and turn into energy, chiefly heat.

Atomic clock

Accurate timekeeping by an atomic clock is based on the regular vibrations of atoms.

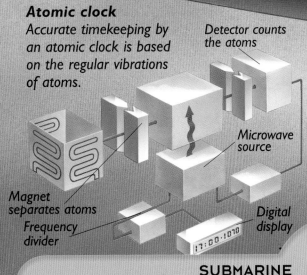

Detector counts the atoms

Microwave source

Magnet separates atoms

Frequency divider

Digital display

17:00:1070

SUBMARINE

Rotor and stator

The main parts of the generator are two huge sets of wire coils, the rotor and stator. The rotor spins or revolves inside the stator, which remains stationary.

Contacts

Each sliding electrical contact consists of a metallic strip on the shaft of the generator, and a brush that touches it as the shaft rotates. The brush is usually made of a composite material containing carbon, so that it carries electricity but causes little wear or friction. This arrangement is needed to conduct electric current into the fast-spinning coils of the rotor.

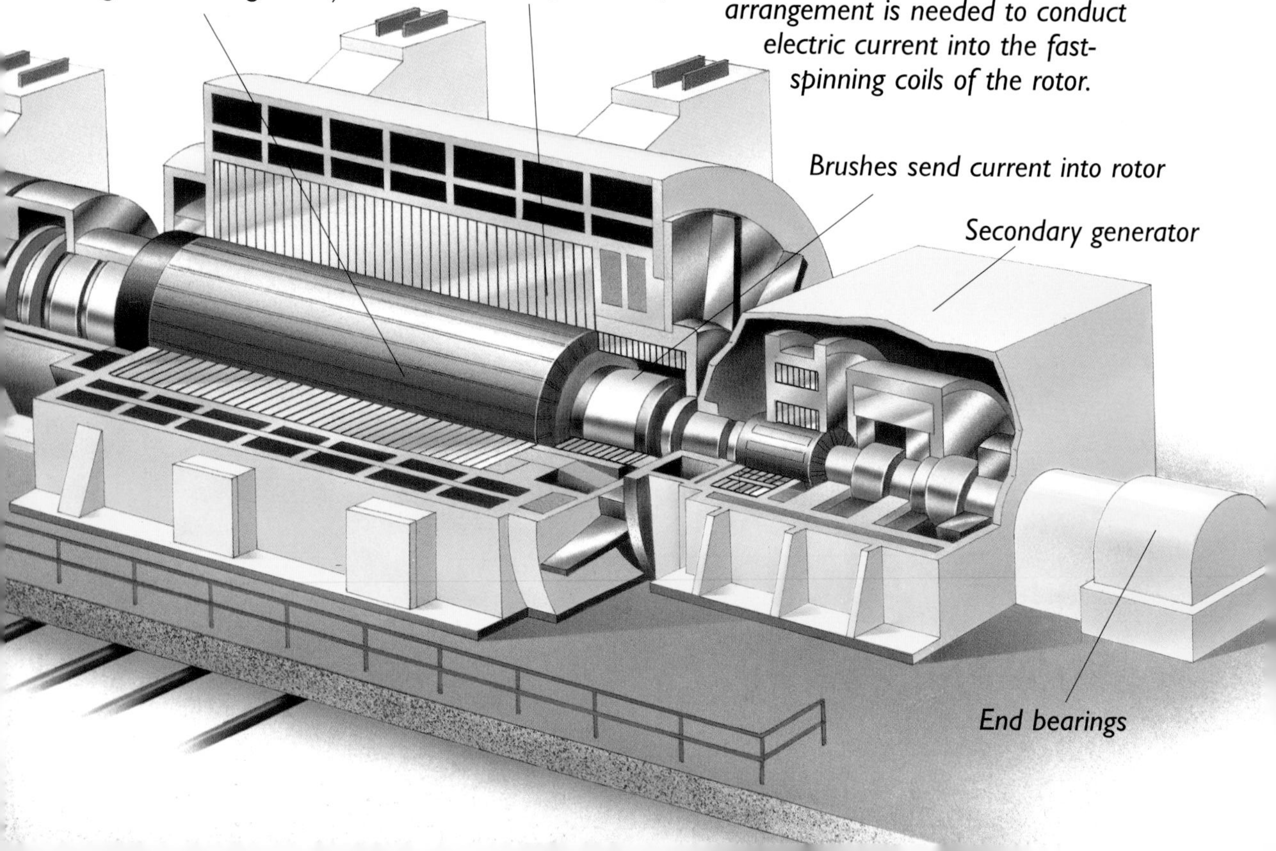

Rotor (spinning coils of wire that use electricity to generate magnetism)

Stator (stationary coils of wire where current is generated)

Brushes send current into rotor

Secondary generator

End bearings

Generators

A generator changes the energy of movement, kinetic energy, into electrical energy. It uses a feature of magnetism and electricity called electromagnetic induction. When a wire moves within a magnetic field, or when a magnetic field moves past a wire, electric current is generated in the wire. In a typical generator, coils of wire spin within powerful magnetic fields, and the electricity generated in them is led away. Electromagnetic induction is the 'opposite' of the electromagnetic effect, where the flow of electricity in a wire produces a magnetic field around the wire.

Solar problems

The Sun's light and heat vary greatly depending on weather and other conditions. They are also very weak in many colder parts of the world, and are absent at night. So solar power has only a limited capacity to generate electricity. Much research continues on industrial methods of storing electricity, in a giant version of a rechargeable car battery, which would help to even out supplies.

Chemical generators

Electricity is generated by chemical reactions, in an electrical cell. A group of cells forms a battery. The first battery was developed by Italian scientist Alessandro Volta (1745-1827) in about 1799. It was a pile of alternating silver and zinc discs with card soaked in salt water between them.

Solar power

By far the greatest source of energy near our world is the Sun. Its light or heat can be captured and used to generate electricity, by a solar power station.

POWER AND STRENGTH

Kepler and his laws

The laws of planetary motion were discovered by German astronomer Johann Kepler, between 1608 and 1619. He worked out that Earth and the other planets do not travel in exact circles around the Sun. They move in oval-like shapes called ellipses. The Sun is not in the middle of an orbital ellipse, but at one of its twin 'centres', called a focus. Also each planet does not move at a constant speed. It goes faster as it comes nearer the Sun, then slower as it travels away.

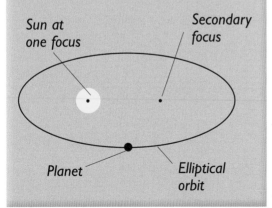

Sun at one focus

Secondary focus

Planet

Elliptical orbit

Round and round

In circular motion, an object stays at a constant distance from one point, the centre, as it moves. This also includes objects that spin or revolve around a central point or line, like a wheel on an axle. Circular motion is not the most 'natural' form of movement – going in a straight line is. For an object to travel in a circle, there must be a force on it, which continuously makes its path move around in a curve. For planets orbiting the Sun, the force is the Sun's gravity.

Binary stars

More than half of all stars are not single, like our Sun, but binaries or multiples – two or more stars very close together. Their motions depend on their sizes. Two similar partners follow each other in circular orbit (1). A much smaller star orbits a huge one (2). Or two dissimilar partners orbit a point between them (3).

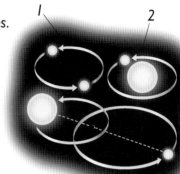

Black hole

A black hole is a place where gigantic amounts of matter are squeezed into an unimaginably small place. Its gravity is so strong and concentrated, nothing can get away – not even light, which is why the hole is black. The gravity pulls planets, stars, gas and dust, which spiral into the hole.

Solar circles

The Sun is a star in the middle of the Solar System. The system consists of nine planets that orbit in ellipses. The four innermost planets are smallish and made mainly of rocks. Our own world, Earth, is among them as 'third rock from the Sun'. After a wide gap populated by even smaller rocky lumps, called asteroids, the next four planets are huge 'gas giants'.

Friction

Friction is 'the enemy of machines'. It changes the energy of motion, kinetic energy, into the energy of heat. Friction is basically rubbing or scraping that causes wear, tear, slowing down and getting hot. No matter how smooth a surface such as polished metal, there are still tiny lumps and bumps, perhaps just a few million atoms high. As another surface slides past, the lumps rub past against each other. Friction can be lessened by using very smooth, almost slip-free substances, and by lubrication such as oil or grease.

Low-friction wheels and bearings on rollercoaster

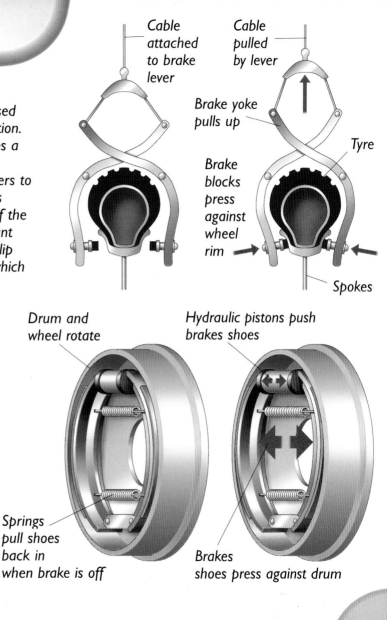

Cable attached to brake lever

Cable pulled by lever

Brake yoke pulls up

Tyre

Brake blocks press against wheel rim

Spokes

Useful friction 1

Friction is very useful when used deliberately, to slow down motion. Pressing the brake lever makes a cable pull on the brake yokes. These swivel like a pair of levers to make the rubber brake blocks press against the metal rim of the wheel. Water acts as a lubricant and allows the wheel rim to slip past the blocks more easily, which is why bicycle brakes are less effective in wet conditions.

Useful friction 2

Car brakes work in a similar way to bicycle brakes, but by hydraulics rather than levers. In a car, curved parts called brake shoes press on the drum-shaped inside part of the wheel, to make the wheel spin more slowly. The covering of the brake shoe becomes very hot and so it must be made from a temperature-resistant composite substance.

Drum and wheel rotate

Hydraulic pistons push brakes shoes

Springs pull shoes back in when brake is off

Brakes shoes press against drum

Old water turbines

The waterwheel of ancient times is a type of turbine. Water flows past the angled blades and pushes them, converting the kinetic energy of its flow into the rotational kinetic energy of the wheel. Waterwheels were used for tasks such as turning millstones to grind cereals to flour.

New water turbines

The modern hydro-electric turbine is an electricity-generating version of the old waterwheel. Water held back by a dam is led along pipes to turn angled turbine blades and a generator.

Spin and shake

A modern generator in a power station is a gigantic machine that must run for years without stopping and with hardly any maintenance. Its rotating parts have to be perfectly balanced in their bearings. Otherwise, as they spin, they would set up vibrations that cause wear, and might eventually create cracks or even shake the device apart. The forces which affect spinning objects are very different from those stressing stationary objects.

Rotating around

Rotary motion is a special type of circular motion. It happens when an object spins or revolves around a central point or line, like a wheel on an axle, or a set of turbine blades on a shaft. Once a wheel is set turning or rotating, it has a tendency to keep turning – a feature known as angular momentum. The heavier the wheel and objects connected to it, the greater the momentum. This effect is used in massive flywheels, which are used to smooth out small fluctuations in rotational speed.

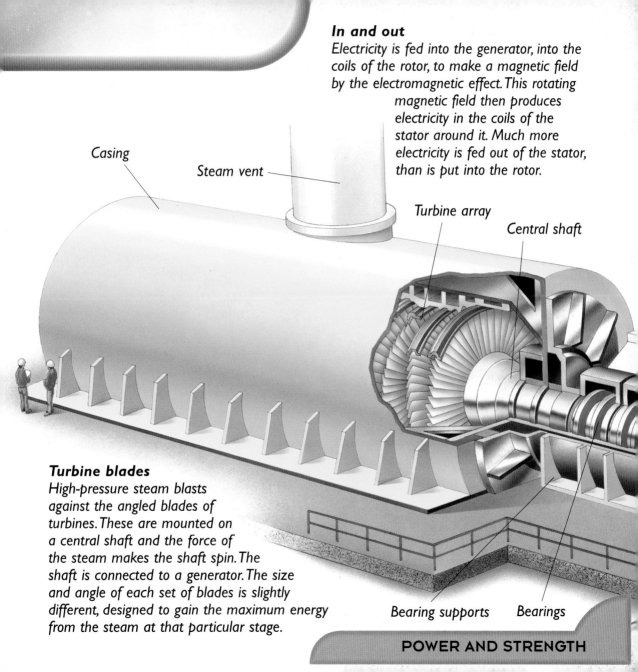

In and out
Electricity is fed into the generator, into the coils of the rotor, to make a magnetic field by the electromagnetic effect. This rotating magnetic field then produces electricity in the coils of the stator around it. Much more electricity is fed out of the stator, than is put into the rotor.

Casing

Steam vent

Turbine array

Central shaft

Turbine blades
High-pressure steam blasts against the angled blades of turbines. These are mounted on a central shaft and the force of the steam makes the shaft spin. The shaft is connected to a generator. The size and angle of each set of blades is slightly different, designed to gain the maximum energy from the steam at that particular stage.

Bearing supports

Bearings

POWER AND STRENGTH

Everything pulls

Gravity is one of the four fundamental forces of the Universe. It is a pulling or attracting force possessed by all objects, from the particles that make up an atom, to a giant star. Earth's gravity pulls all objects towards it, keeping us and them firmly on the surface. To fly into space, a rocket like the space shuttle must get away from the pull of Earth's gravity by moving at a speed called escape velocity, which is 11.2 kilometres per second.

6

5

Escape of the shuttle

From 3.8 seconds before lift-off (1) all three of the shuttle's orbiter engines fire. The solid-fuel boosters begin their burn 2.9 seconds after lift-off (2) The boosters burn out and release at 2 minutes 12 seconds (3) The external fuel tank is empty and released by 8 minutes 50 seconds (4) The shuttle enters Earth orbit soon after (5) and begins its mission (6).

4

3

2

1

Gravity on land

Super-fast cars like the world land speed record-holder, Thrust SSC, cannot rely on gravity to hold them down. They move so rapidly that they may almost take off. Such cars have aerodynamic shapes to help press them down.

Gravity, mass and weight

Every object or substance has mass. This is, in effect, a measure of how many atoms, and which types of atoms, it contains. The mass of an object is the same everywhere. A person has the same mass on Earth, in space and on the Moon. Weight is different. It is produced by the pull of gravity acting on the object, and so depends on gravity. A person with a weight of 60 kilograms on Earth, would weigh about 10 kilograms on the Moon, and be weightless in the zero-gravity conditions of space.

Earth's gravity

Straight line tendency

Orbital path

Gravity in orbit

Isaac Newton showed that an object tends to keep moving in a straight line, at the same speed, unless a force acts on it. A satellite tries to do this, but the force of Earth's gravity pulls it down. The result is a curved path called an orbit, as the satellite goes round and round the Earth.

Ideas about gravity

English scientist Isaac Newton (1642-1727) suggested that gravity was a universal force, possessed by all objects. Earth's gravity not only pulls falling apples down to the ground, it also holds the Moon in orbit around the Earth. Newton's ideas were revised by Albert Einstein (1879-1955).

INTO SPACE

Gears and cogs

Cog wheels have teeth which fit into, or mesh with, similar teeth on another cog wheel. The basic cog wheel set-up can transfer a turning force from one place to another. It can reverse the direction of the turning force, since the driven cog turns in the opposite direction to the driving cog. And depending on the numbers of teeth, a cog system can speed up or slow the rate of rotation, and reduce or increase the turning power.

Winding mechanism coils spring

Gears on the wrist

A wristwatch gains its energy from a spiral spring which is wound up. The spring's tension is allowed to reduce very slowly by a system of tiny cogs and other gear-type mechanisms. These miniature mechanical devices sometimes have jewelled or diamond bearings, for long life.

Types of cogs and gears

Cogs or teeth are carefully designed so that they fit very closely, without too much rubbing or sloppiness. This reduces wear and also transfers as much force as smoothly as possible.

Simple cogs reverse direction of rotation

Rack

Bevels move direction of rotation through a right angle (90°)

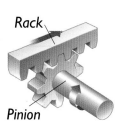

Pinion

Worm

Winch

A typical electric winch has a motor that rotates rapidly. A system of gears greatly slows down this turning speed, but at the same time, greatly increases its force. The result is that a rollercoaster car full of people can be winched by a driving cog, meshed into a slotted chain, up a very steep slope.

Low and high gears

In low gearing, like the rollercoaster winch, the driving cog turns many times compared to a few turns of the driven cog. But the turning force, or torque, is greatly increased. In a high gear, the opposite occurs. The driven cog rotates very fast but its torque is decreased.

Winch and gearing mechanism under car

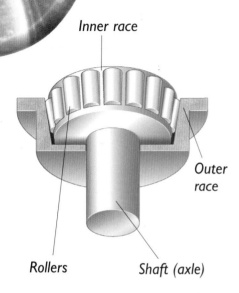

Inner race

Outer race

Rollers

Shaft (axle)

Smooth motion

A bearing is designed to allow one part, like a wheel, to move against another part, such as an axle, with the least rubbing or friction. The ball-bearing is one of the strongest, most hard-wearing, and most effective designs. All the parts are made of very hard, smooth metal, usually a type of steel. They are lubricated with grease or oil. A mirror-ball or a spotlight such as a follow-spot must move smoothly, without jerks, to follow the performers as they travel around the stage. So it is usually mounted on a ball-bearing.

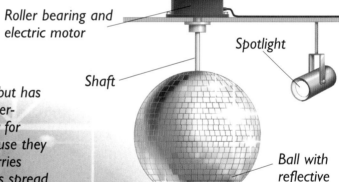

Roller bearing and electric motor

Shaft

Spotlight

Ball with reflective mirrors

Roller-bearing

This bearing is similar to a ball-bearing, but has rollers shaped like rods or cones. The roller-bearing is used for heavier machinery or for bearing which must be long-lasting because they are in inaccessible places. Each roller carries weight along its length. So the pressure is spread out more, compared to a ball-bearing where it is concentrated into spots.

Lots of energy

A stadium show emits many forms of energy — especially sound from the loudspeakers, and light and heat from the lighting system. There are also radio waves from the cordless radio-microphones.

Electric motor

Thousands of machines are driven by electric motors. They are generally quiet, safe, smooth-running and easily controlled and very efficent. They change more than nine-tenths of the energy supplied to them, as electricity, into the energy of rotary motion

Rolling and pulling

The wheel is one of the simplest machines, and one of most common. It is like a never-ending inclined plane (slope or ramp) wrapped around a central point, the axle. A wheel reduces the slowing effect of friction hugely, by allowing an object to roll across a surface, rather than being dragged. The wheels do use up some energy, as their edge or rim presses down on the surface. This rolling resistance increases as the wheel's edge, and/or the surface, become less smooth. A pulley is a wheel with a grooved or dished rim. It turns to allow a rope or cable to move past it.

Easing the load

Groups or blocks of pulleys can help to lift heavy loads more easily. One rope or cable passes up and down, around alternate pulleys in the upper and lower blocks. When the rope is wound in, it lifts the load more easily than without pulleys. But more rope has to be wound in, to move the load only a short distance. In this respect, a pulley system is like a lever. A small effort moves a big load, but not very far.

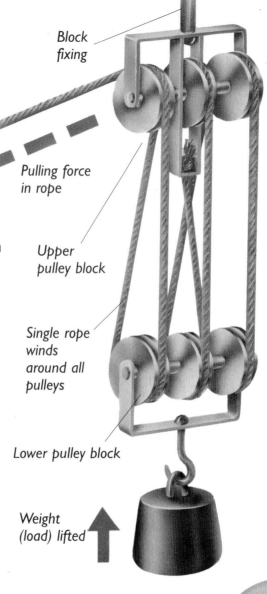

Block fixing

Pulling force in rope

Upper pulley block

Single rope winds around all pulleys

Lower pulley block

Weight (load) lifted

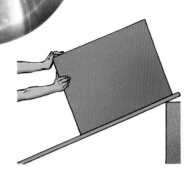

Inclined plane

This is a slope or ramp. It allows an object to be lifted or moved in small, continuous amounts, rather than in one large step.

Wedge

Made of two inclined planes, back to back, the wedge can force two objects apart. Or, in the case of an axe or chisel blade, split an object.

Screw

A wedge, twisted like a corkscrew around a central rod, forms a screw. It converts a turning force into a straight-line movement.

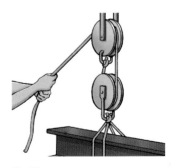

Lever

A rigid bar tilts on a pivot, or fulcrum. A small force at one end produces a large force at the other end.

Wheel and axle

The wheel is like one curved, never-ending inclined plane, wrapped around a central point. It changes sliding or rubbing into rolling.

Pulley

A rope or cable passes round a wheel with a dished rim. Pulleys change the direction of a pulling force or convert it to rotary motion.

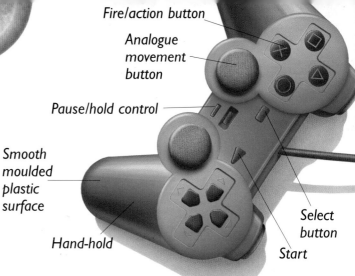

Fire/action button

Analogue movement button

Pause/hold control

Smooth moulded plastic surface

Select button

Start

Hand-hold

Joypad

The switches and buttons are made of plastic and are impact-resistant. They have intricate shapes – features which would be difficult to obtain with other materials, such as wood or glass.

Basic mechanics

Mechanical devices work using physically moving parts, unlike electrical, hydraulic (liquid-based), pneumatic (air), acoustic (sound) or optical (light) systems. Most mechanical devices are built up from combinations of a few very simple machines. These include the inclined plane (ramp), wedge, lever, screw, wheel and axle, and pulley. In daily life, many devices are combinations of these different systems. The handset for a games console has mechanical components and also electrical ones.

Rocker lever

A rocker switch in a joypad works like a lever. The switch is a shaped bar that pivots on its hinge, or fulcrum. There are electrical contacts at one end in the switch and the base. Pressing one end of the switch brings the contacts together so electricity can flow and the switch is ON. Pressing the other end makes the switch flick to OFF.

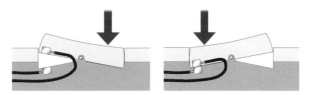

Types of levers

A rocker switch works as two types of lever, depending on the relative positions of the effort (the pressing finger), fulcrum, and load (the contacts). Each type has certain advantages.

Liquid pressure

Machines that work using liquids are known as hydraulic devices. Most liquids cannot be made smaller, or compressed. So when a liquid is put under pressure, it carries or transmits the pressure evenly, throughout itself. Push the liquid at one end of a pipe, and the liquid exerts this pressure all along the walls of the pipe, and at the other end too. Hydraulic machines use pipes, pistons, cylinders and other devices to produce a movement in one place, using pressure at another place, and to increase or decrease pressure.

Gyroscope

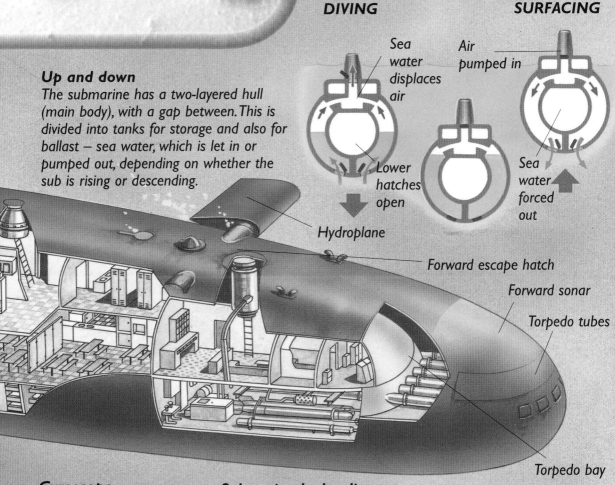

DIVING

Sea water displaces air

Lower hatches open

SURFACING

Air pumped in

Sea water forced out

Up and down

The submarine has a two-layered hull (main body), with a gap between. This is divided into tanks for storage and also for ballast – sea water, which is let in or pumped out, depending on whether the sub is rising or descending.

Hydroplane

Forward escape hatch

Forward sonar

Torpedo tubes

Torpedo bay

Gyroscope

Submarines use gyroscopes for navigation and to stay steady in rough seas and strong currents. The gyro has a wheel which spins fast and stays steady.

Submarine hydraulics

A submarine has dozens of hydraulic devices, connected by pipes of pressurized oil. The hydroplanes at the front of the vessel, and the rudders at the rear, are tilted up and down by hydraulic pistons, on their shafts inside the sub's hull. Hydroplanes make the front angle up for surfacing.

SUBMARINE

Energy of vibrations

Sound waves are to-and-fro movements or vibrations in a substance, rippling outwards from a source. The vibrations gradually fade as their energy spreads and weakens. Sounds pass through gases, liquids and solids. We usually hear sounds that travel through gases (air). Sounds move more rapidly, for longer distances, through liquids. They go even faster and farther in solids. Because sound energy needs atoms for its passage it cannot travel through a vacuum such as space.

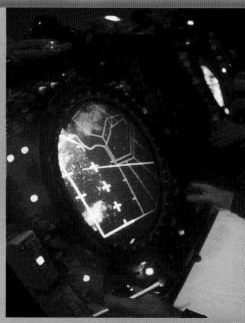

Sonar

Ships use sonar (SOund Navigation And Ranging), or echo-sounding, to detect objects in the water, including the sea bed. Powerful pulses or 'pings' of sound from an emitter are reflected or bounced back as echoes. These are detected, analyzed by computer and displayed on a screen.

Radar

Radar is the radio-wave version of sonar (left). Radio waves are sent into the sky where objects such as planes, clouds and tall buildings reflect them back, for detection and analysis. Results are usually updated every few seconds and displayed on a screen. Radar is especially useful for air traffic control, to track aircraft around an airport, and to detect clouds for weather forecasting.

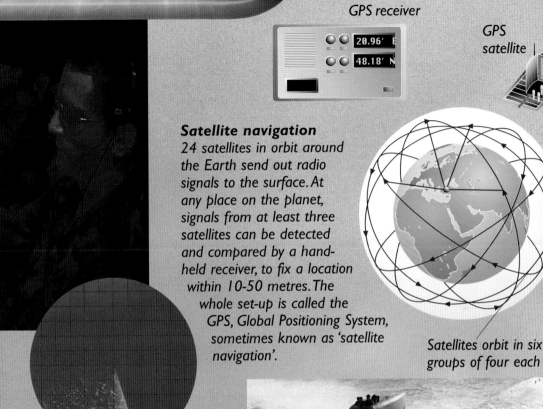

GPS receiver

20.96' E
48.18' N

GPS satellite

Satellite navigation

24 satellites in orbit around the Earth send out radio signals to the surface. At any place on the planet, signals from at least three satellites can be detected and compared by a hand-held receiver, to fix a location within 10-50 metres. The whole set-up is called the GPS, Global Positioning System, sometimes known as 'satellite navigation'.

Satellites orbit in six groups of four each

Direction and ranging

In sonar, the direction from which echoes return shows the direction of the object. Also sound's speed in water is known, so the time taken for a sound pulse to travel to the object and back again, shows the range — the distance to the object.

SUBMARINE

Seeking heat

Some types of missiles search out their target by sensing the heat energy that it gives off. Both jet and propeller planes have engines which leave an invisible trail of hot gases behind them as they fly. The missile's sensors 'scan' the sky and detect this heat by the rays it emits, which are called infra-red waves. The missile then locks onto the heat trail and follows it right up to the engine's exhaust.

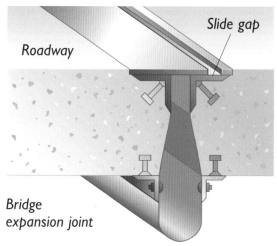

Roadway

Slide gap

Bridge
expansion joint

Expansion problems

Many machines, engines and structures have metal parts, and most metals expand as they become warm. Hot weather can cause problems for metal bridges and railway lines, as they grow in length. So gaps or sliding joints are designed to allow for this.

How heat moves: 1

Heat energy moves in three main ways. As atoms and molecules become warmer, they vibrate more, bump into atoms and molecules around them, and set them vibrating too. Gradually the vibrations spread through a substance. This is thermal conduction.

Hot coffee conducts heat to cup

Getting bigger

The form of energy called heat is based on the movements of atoms and molecules in a substance. These do not stay still, even in a solid. They move or vibrate around a central area. In a very cold substance, these vibrations are small. As energy is supplied to the atoms and molecules, they move more, and faster. The substance gets hotter, and also larger, which is known as thermal expansion. If the supply of energy ceases, then as the heat energy is given off, the substance cools down and shrinks or contracts.

How heat moves: 2 and 3

As a substance becomes hot and expands, its atoms and molecules move slightly farther apart. The substance becomes less dense. If it is a region of a liquid or gas, and can flow, it rises above its cooler, denser surroundings, carrying heat with it. This is convection. A third way in which heat moves is radiation, as infra-red rays (part of the EM spectrum of rays and waves). These can travel through space – it's how the Sun keeps us warm.

Hot gases blast from a jet engine and then rise through the cold air around them, by convection.

Waves we can see

Light is one way in which energy moves from place to place. Light waves are similar in nature to radio waves, microwaves and X-rays. They are a form of energy called electromagnetic (EM) radiation. This consists of a combination of electricity and magnetism, becoming stronger in peaks, then weaker in troughs, in a wave-like fashion. Light and all other forms of EM waves travel at the same speed, which we usually call the speed of light. This is about 300,000 kilometres per second (which is a million times faster than sound waves).

Pieces of light

Swiss-American scientist Albert Einstein (1879-1955) is remembered mainly for his work on the theory of relativity. But before this, he also worked on light. At the time, light was regarded only as waves. Einstein went back to a much

older idea, that light might also be viewed as units or particles, called photons. In 1905 he explained how light can be converted into electricity.

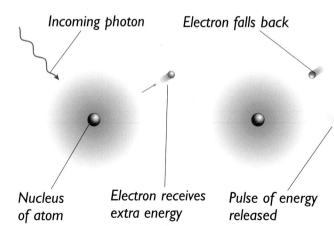

Incoming photon

Electron falls back

Nucleus of atom

Electron receives extra energy

Pulse of energy released

Waves and particles

Light can be viewed as tiny packets of energy, photons. When one hits a certain type of atom, it gives the atom extra energy, which can make one of the atom's electrons jump into a different position. Later, when the electron jumps back, the atom gives out a burst of energy. This may be light or some other form, such as X-rays or radio waves.

Colours of light

Light waves have a range of lengths, although all are very short, with thousands of waves stretching only one millimetre. We see the longest light waves as the colour red, medium-length ones as green, and the shortest light waves as blue and violet. All of these different colours make up the visible spectrum of light – 'the colours of the rainbow'.

Inventing light

Electricity can be changed into light by many devices. The commonest one is the light bulb. An early type of light bulb was developed in 1879 by American inventor and engineer, Thomas Edison (1847-1931).
His team of workers tested more than 4000 substances which glowed white-hot when electricity passed through them. Edison also invented an early type of sound recorder-player, called the phonograph, and a kind of microphone.

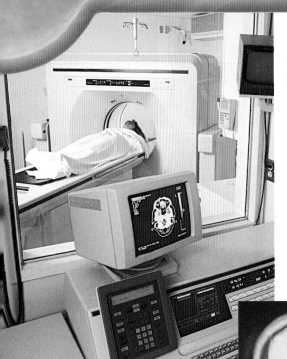

Radioactivity

Radioactivity is a particular type of energy which is given off, or radiated, by the nuclei (centres) of certain atoms. It may be very harmful to living things, including the human body. Radioactivity is produced by the breakdown, or decay, of nuclei which are unbalanced or unstable for some reason. As the nuclei decay they give off three possible kinds of radioactivity, called alpha, beta and gamma. Although radioactivity may be harmful, it can also be used in medicine to treat disease.

Seeing disease

Tiny, harmless amounts of radioactivity can help to pinpoint diseased parts. A biochemical substance that is taken up by a certain part of the body is made radioactive, and then put into the body, by injection or being eaten. A special radioactivity-sensing scanner or camera takes pictures of where the substance is concentrated. Unusual amounts or sites indicate problems such as tumours.

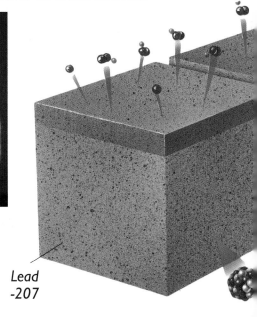

Lead -207

Types of radioactivity

There are three main kinds of radioactivity. Alpha rays are actually particles, each containing two protons and two neutrons. Beta rays are also particles, usually fast-moving electrons. Gamma rays are waves of EM (electromagnetic) energy, similar to light rays and X-rays, but the lengths of the waves are very short.

Radiotherapy

The harmful effects of radioactivity can be harnessed as radiotherapy. For example, in a brain tumour, cells multiply out of control. A small pellet of radioactive substance put into the site can send out enough radioactivity to damage the cells of the tumour around it, but not healthy tissues farther away.

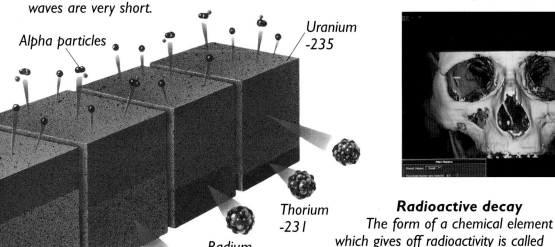

Alpha particles

Uranium -235

Thorium -231

Radium -227

Radon -223

Polonium -219

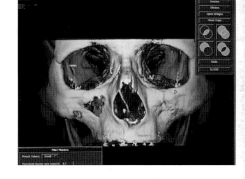

Radioactive decay

The form of a chemical element which gives off radioactivity is called its radio-isotope. For elements with very large nuclei, like uranium and radium, all forms are radio-isotopes. As the nuclei decay, giving off waves and particles, they change into other elements. This happens at a constant rate, through various stages, until a stable end product is reached. Uranium-235 gradually decays into lead-207.

HUMAN BODY

Invisible power

Switch on a portable radio set, anywhere in the world, and you can tune into a programme. Radio waves are always all around us. They are a form of EM (electromagnetic) energy, similar in nature to light waves, and travelling at the same speed. But, of course, radio waves are invisible. They vary in length from several kilometres for a single wave, to about one metre per wave. Radio waves are produced by a radio transmitter, when an electric current changes direction, or oscillates, very quickly. Natural objects like lightning and stars in space also produce radio waves.

Receiving the Universe

Radio waves come from a variety of objects deep in space, such as stars, galaxies, quasars and the edges of black holes. The waves are very faint, so they are collected by huge antennae shaped like dishes or bowls. These are called radio-telescopes. Here on Earth, our own radio waves can be altered, or modulated, to carry information. The alterations may be in the heights of the waves (amplitude modulation, AM). Or they are in the number of waves per second (frequency modulation, FM).

Receiving radio

The shape of an antenna affects how it detects radio signals.

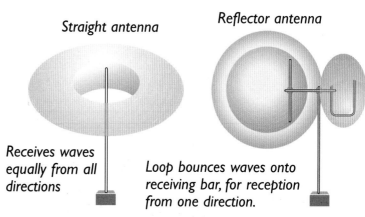

Straight antenna

Reflector antenna

Receives waves equally from all directions

Loop bounces waves onto receiving bar, for reception from one direction.

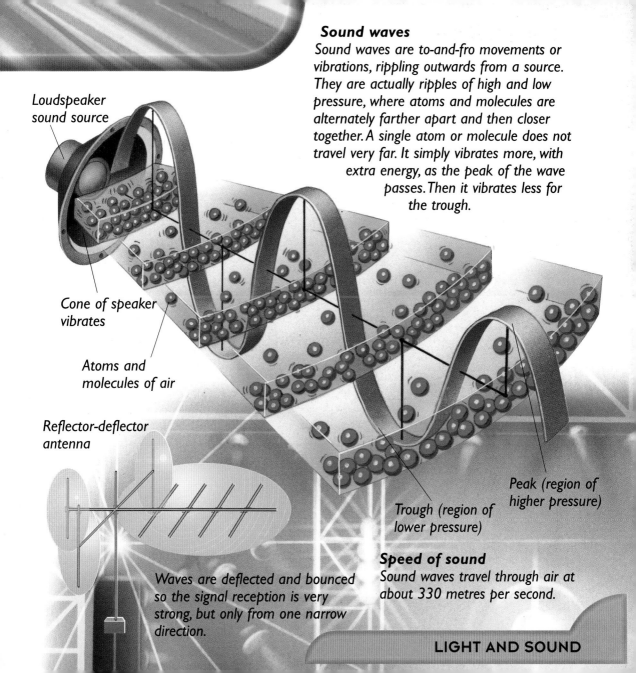

Sound waves

Sound waves are to-and-fro movements or vibrations, rippling outwards from a source. They are actually ripples of high and low pressure, where atoms and molecules are alternately farther apart and then closer together. A single atom or molecule does not travel very far. It simply vibrates more, with extra energy, as the peak of the wave passes. Then it vibrates less for the trough.

Loudspeaker
sound source

Cone of speaker
vibrates

Atoms and
molecules of air

Reflector-deflector
antenna

Peak (region of
higher pressure)

Trough (region of
lower pressure)

Waves are deflected and bounced so the signal reception is very strong, but only from one narrow direction.

Speed of sound

Sound waves travel through air at about 330 metres per second.

LIGHT AND SOUND

Very short waves

X-rays were discovered in 1895 by German physics professor Wilhelm Roentgen. He did not understand their nature, so he called them X-rays, 'X' for 'unknown'. They are now known to be similar in nature to radio waves and light rays – electromagnetic (EM) waves composed of ripples of electrical and magnetic energy. However the waves of X-rays are incredibly short in length, much shorter than light waves. About 10 million X-rays in a row would stretch only one millimetre.

X-rated mystery

At Würzburg, Wilhelm Roentgen (1845-1923) was carrying out experiments with a discharge tube. This passes high-voltage electricity through a vacuum or certain gases. He noticed that a nearby piece of card coated with a barium-containing chemical glowed when the tube was switched on. Roentgen guessed the tube gave off previously unknown waves, which for a time were called Roentgen rays, but we now know them as X-rays.

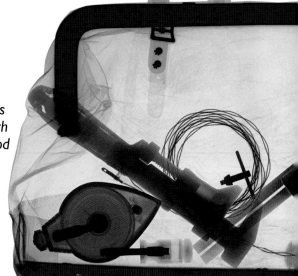

See-through rays

X-rays are powerful and penetrating, which means they pass straight through substances like card, wood and the flesh of the body. They are stopped by harder, heavier, denser substances such as teeth and lead.

How an x-ray machine works

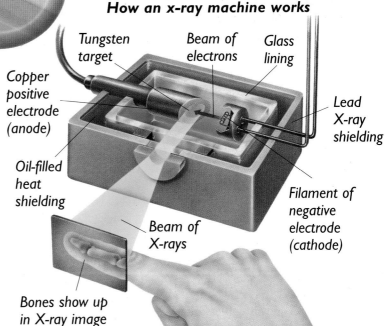

Tungsten target

Beam of electrons

Glass lining

Copper positive electrode (anode)

Lead X-ray shielding

Oil-filled heat shielding

Filament of negative electrode (cathode)

Beam of X-rays

Bones show up in X-ray image

Making X-rays

In one type of X-ray machine, electricity at 100,000 volts is passed between two electrodes. The electricity is in the usual form of electrons. They flow from the negative electrode, which is a very hot, glowing filament of wire, across a gap to the positive electrode, which is a massive copper block to absorb heat. The electrons hit a small 'target' of the metal tungsten, at such high speed that X-rays are given off.

Using X-rays

X-rays can be harmful to living things, including people. They cause sickness, burns and long-term problems such as cancers. However the X-rays used to show parts of the body, such as teeth and bones, are very weak. X-rays can also see inside cases and bags, outlining metals and similar substances.

Teeth and jaw bones show clearly as white in this OPT dental X-ray

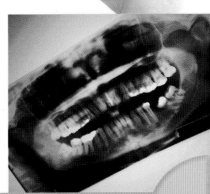

ATOMS IN ACTION

Lots of waves

Space is full of waves. Many objects there give off vast quantities of energy in the form of electromagnetic or EM radiation. A gigantic source of such energy which is relatively close to Earth, is the Sun. It sends out light, heat, ultra-violet and other electromagnetic waves, which radiate in all directions, and take about eight minutes to reach Earth. The waves are collectively known as solar radiation. Other objects in space send out powerful bursts of radio waves and gamma waves.

Background radiation

The COBE satellite (COsmic Background Explorer), launched in 1989, carried delicate sensors for microwaves. It discovered that microwaves are passing evenly in all directions through the Universe. This supports the idea that the Universe began in a gigantic explosion, billions of years ago. The microwaves are often called the 'echoes' or 'afterglow' of the Big Bang.

Sensing waves

Hundreds of artificial or man-made satellites have been launched into space by rocket engines. The satellites detect various kinds of EM waves, such as light, infra-red, ultra-violet and microwaves. These come up from Earth and also travel through space from faraway stars, galaxies and other objects.

Satellite photograph of volcanic mountains in Ecuador

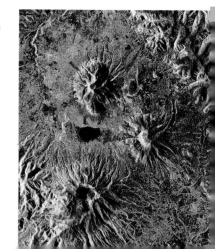

Cosmic 'rays'

Cosmic rays are not EM radiation, but a mix of high-energy particles travelling through space. They mostly collide with atoms of gas in Earth's atmosphere.

Sun's electromagnetic radiation

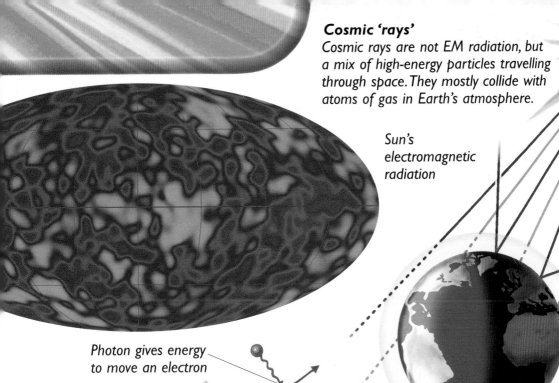

Photon gives energy to move an electron

Photons (particles of light energy) hit junction between layers

Making light work

A photovoltaic cell changes light energy into an electric current. It consists of a sandwich of substances called semiconductors, such as silicon. Cells are grouped together into solar arrays or panels and used to power many devices, from calculators to satellites.

The EM spectrum

Many kinds of rays and waves have the same basic form. They are ripples of electrical and magnetic energy, known as electromagnetic waves. They all travel at the same speed, which is named after one of the best-known types of EM waves, light. The speed of light is about 300,000 kilometres per second. Unlike sound waves, EM waves do not need atoms to travel. So they can pass through the nothingness of a vacuum.

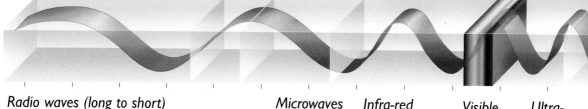

Radio waves (long to short)   Microwaves   Infra-red waves   Visible light   Ultra-violet

Visible light

Most camera films are sensitive to the visible light part of the EM spectrum.

Infra-red

Waves of the infra-red type carry heat energy with them. We feel the infra-red rays as warmth. Certain types of screens or camera films are sensitive, not to light rays, but to infra-red waves.

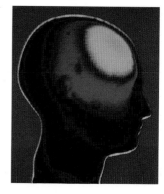

Ultra-violet

Waves of the ultra-violet length can be detected by certain kinds of camera film, and tend to show up in shades, of blue, purple, indigo and violet. Ultra-violet rays from the Sun can cause sunburn.

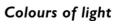

White light   Prism   Spectrum of colours ('rainbow')

Colours of light

We see each length of light wave as a certain colour. Longest are red, medium are green, and shortest are violet. All of these mixed form 'white' light.

X-rays   Gamma rays

Primary colours of light

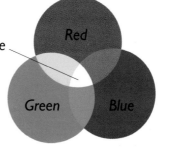

White

Red

Green   Blue

Primary colours of pigments

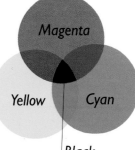

Magenta

Yellow   Cyan

Black

Length and frequency

Along the EM spectrum, the waves gradually become shorter. In 'long wave' radio they are many kilometres in length. Microwaves are generally from one metre to about one millimetre long. Gamma rays have a wavelength of billionths of a millimetre. As wavelengths decrease, their frequency – the number of waves going past in one second – increases.

Colours

When mixing light of different colours, the colours add together. Red, green and blue contain most of the wavelengths of light and mix to make white. The coloured substances called pigments, used in paints and dyes, take away light and mix to make black.

FUN WITH SCIENCE

GLOSSARY

Alloy A mixture of two or more metals, or a metal and a non-metal.

Atom The smallest part of an element.

Catalyst A substance that improves the rate of a chemical reaction, remaining unchanged itself.

Combustion A chemical reaction in which a substance combines with oxygen and gives off heat and light.

Conduction The process that allows heat to be transferred from one part of a substance to another.

Convection The movement of molecules from a warmer place to a cooler place ie in liquid or gas.

Electrolysis The passing of electricity through a liquid that contains ions in order to produce a chemical reaction.

Expansion The process by which a substance, remaining the same in mass, increases in volume.

Force The push or pull that makes something move, slows it down or stops it, or the pressure that something exerts on an object.

Friction A force that is created when a solid object rubs against another or when it moves through a liquid or gas.

Gravity The force that pulls objects towards the ground.

Ion An atom that has lost or gained electrons and carries an electrical charge.

Magnetic field An area around the poles of a magnet, in which the magnet can exert a force.

Mass The amount of material an object contains. An object's mass never changes. Its weight depends on gravity.

Molecule The smallest amount of a chemical substance that can exist alone, which is made up of two or more atoms.

Plasma An electrically charged gas made up of equal numbers of positive ions and free electrons.

Photosynthesis The process by which green plants make food from carbon dioxide and water.

Pressure The force applied to a certain area.

Radioactivity The emission of radiation from unstable elements by the splitting of their atomic nuclei.

Vacuum A region in which there is no matter.

INDEX